Purl SOHO

CREATE | SHOP

www.purlsoho.com

Cover Image Vytoky cultural project introduced by Ukrainian Fashion Week photographer Dmitry Komissarenko

Selvedge Magazine
Editorial Office
162 Archway Road, London N6 5BB
editor@selvedge.org www.selvedge.org
T: +44 (0)20 8341 9721

Publisher: Selvedge Ltd

Founder: Polly Leonard editor@selvedge.org
Features Editor: Grace Warde-Aldam editorial@selvedge.org
Copy Editor: Peter Shaw

Head of Communications: Clare Bungey communications@selvedge.org
Events Director: Penny Gray events@selvedge.org
Community Manager: Emma Neen promotions@selvedge.org
Distribution Manager: Ronja Brown distributions@selvedge.org
Workshop Assistant: Jessica Edney saturday@selvedge.org
Interns: Ailish Reaney & Lottie Hampson intern@selvedge.org

selvedge

SELVEDGE (ISSN: 1742-254X) is published bi-monthly six times a year in January, March, May, July, September and November by Selvedge Ltd. Registered Office 14 Milton Park, Highgate, London, N6 5QA. Copyright © Selvedge Ltd 2016. All rights reserved. Reproduction in whole or in part without written permission is strictly prohibited. The editor reserves the right to edit, shorten or modify any material submitted. The editor's decision on all printed material is final. The views expressed by contributors are not necessarily those of Selvedge magazine, Selvedge Ltd or the editor. Unsolicited material will be considered but cannot be returned. Printing: Westdale Press Ltd UK. Colour Origination: PH Media. Web Design: datadial. Distribution: Spatial Mail. Postmaster send address corrections to Selvedge Magazine, Spatial House, Willow Farm Business Park, Castle Donnington, Derby, DE74 2TW. Subscription rates for one year (6 issues): Paper Magazine, UK £50.00; Europe £75.00; USA & Rest of World £100.00

BIAS

On bitterly-cold January mornings the need for performance fibres is as clear as the blue sky. Cashmere, Vicuna, Alpaca and Goose Down – all words we associate with luxury and indulgence. I would, however, argue that they are not a luxury but a practical necessity. In this issue we explore the fibres native to extreme locations where wild weather is the norm. Here our designers are looking to nature and science for the answer to lightweight warmth.

We journey as far afield as the Mongolian steppes with Tengari and Norlha founded on the Tibetan plateau, Denis Colomb cashmere from Nepal, June Cashmere from Kyrgyzstan as well as Thibault Van Der Straete's Andean alpaca. Each niche fibre has unique qualities; cashmere is eight times warmer than sheep's wool and does not pill or wrinkle. Alpaca is three times warmer than sheep's wool – and with no lanolin, less itchy but also water-repellent. We explore fibres that wick moisture away from the body; hollow fibres that insulate; and fibres that come in a myriad of different natural shades alleviating the need for dyes. What is important about these fibres is their variety – best explored through the fingers – each one a perfect match for a specific function. These are fibres to cherish, particularly when 85% of all clothing is made from cotton.

Predominantly enjoyed in their natural state, we see an exception in the collection of Moncler, who combine goose down and fur with traditional Tyrolian embroidery. In the darkest days of winter, we long for colour and light. Some of our favourite designers have injected florals into their winter collections. These dramatic dark florals have a jewel-like intensity and a romance not seen in their summer sisters. Originating in Scandinavia with the work of Josef Frank whose exhibition *Patterns-Furniture-Painting* can be seen at the Fashion and Textile Museum, they are the ideal way to brighten up a dark day.

Polly Leonard, Founder

CONTRIBUTORS
We asked our contributors: How far have textiles taken them?

BRYAN ALEXANDER P46

I have been documenting the cultures of the native peoples of northern Siberia since 1992. Siberia is vast and this quest has involved travelling thousands of miles by plane, helicopter, tank, boat, reindeer sledge and dog teams. Although the design of northern Siberia's native clothing varies depending on culture and region, but they use many of the same materials, particularly reindeer skin. I am impressed by the work that goes into making these clothes. They are not only beautiful, but supremely functional in the coldest of Siberian winters.

JESSICA HEMMINGS P64

I travelled overland from Kathmandu to Lhasa when I was twenty and still remember a small carpet patterned with light blue and white squares that I had every intention of buying. The overland road back to Nepal washed out and while stranded in Lhasa I over-stayed my Tibetan visa. Not good. All my spare spending money went to a rather unscrupulous travel agent and, eventually, a flight out – but without that carpet tucked under my arm. I've long since hunted for a surrogate to no avail.

ANNE LAURE CAMILLERI P60

Textiles are an unparalleled way to explore cultures and meet craftspeople around the world. Traditional textiles have taken me to spectacular studios and hot and dusty workshops off the beaten path in Bali, Yogyakarta, Laos, Cambodia, North Carolina, Wisconsin and recently to the White Earth Nation in Northern Minnesota. I'm in awe of the spinners, weavers, dyers and designers who work hard to preserve their crafts while facing harsh competition from mass-produced textiles. Following the textile trail is always a humbling and enriching experience.

CONTENTS

p20/21

p26/27

p36/37

p 40/41

EVENTS dates for your diary

AS YOU SEW – SEW SHALL YOU REAP: *Re-cycle, Re-use and Re-think Textile production,* A symposium in association with Bucks New University, 15 July
ETHEL MAIRET LIVING LEGACY: *Natural dyeing and weaving masterclass* at Ditchling Museum of Art + Craft, 3-7 April
SPRING FAIR The Bath Assembly Rooms, Bennett St, Bath BA1 2QH, 25 March
SUMMER FAIR The Dovecot, 10 Infirmary St, Edinburgh EH1 1LT, 19 August
AUTUMN FAIR Charleston, Firle, Lewes, East Sussex, BN8 6L

WIN gifts and offers for our readers

80 SUBSCRIPTION OFFERS This issue the first 100 three-year subscribers will receive pieces from Kaffe Fassett's cosmetics range, together worth £53
83 PRIZES THIS ISSUE A chance to win a wool and silk Botanical Inlay shawl, worth £125 along with a hand-beaten brass Wall Sconce by Malin Appelgren, worth £265 and a print from the 17th Century Paint Chart, from the Shop Floor Project: www.theshopfloorproject.com; A kindling basket made by Annemarie O'Sullivan, worth £310, www.annemarieosullivan.co.uk; A throw from Tengri, worth £225, www.tengri.co.uk

INFORM the latest news, reviews and exhibition listings

SELVEDGE ('selnid3) n. 1. finished differently 2. the non-fraying edge of a length of woven fabric. [: from SELF + EDGE]

HAND & LOCK
Celebrating 250 Years of Embroidery

Hand & Lock Celebrate 250 Years of Embroidery

Hand & Lock have been producing the world's finest hand embroidery since 1767, specialising in embroidery for the military, the Royal Family, global fashion houses and privat commissions.

In 2017, Hand & Lock will be celebrating 250 years of embroidery with a series of special conferences and exhibitions in Sydney, Chicago and London. The three cities represent embroidery in the 21st century as a business, art form and passion. The conference will consist of must-see talks from international expert speakers. Business leaders, fashion historians, trend predictors, artists and designers will discuss the lessons of the past, challenges of the present and opportunities for the future.

The conference 'Heritage, The Now and The Future of Embroidery' will feature a panel talk, expert guest speakers and an interactive Q&A session. The 'Heritage' talk will look at the nuanced history of embroidery and how the practice impacted and intertwined different disciplines. The 'Now' section will explore the business of contemporary embroidery and the challenges it may face today. The 'Future' will attempt to predict the impact technology and globalisation will have on the practice.

In each city, a touring exhibit will be present and will highlight Hand & Lock's role at the forefront of fashion and military embroidery for the last 250 years, showcase drafts, samples as well as historical ledgers from private archives. In addition, the exhibitions will include a special exhibit featuring specially commissioned unique designer bags embellished in an array of techniques.

In keeping with Hand & Lock's commitment to education, a three day course in Haute Couture Tambour Beading will be taught. This ancient embroidery skill is prized in the world of high fashion as the best way to embellish garments with speed and precision and still used today in European fashion houses.

As the world's oldest embroidery house, Hand & Lock pride themselves in preserving the art form and keeping the tradition of embroidery alive in today's contemporary fashion, ecclesiastical and military work using historical techniques. Not only craftsmen and women, Hand & Lock endeavours to promote the fine art of embroidery and are committed to inspiring the next generation of embroiderers.

Since 2001, Hand & Lock have promoted a programme of embroidery education by creating the annual international embroidery competition 'The Hand & Lock Prize for Embroidery' and also establishing the 'Hand & Lock School for Embroidery' which now operates workshops around the world teaching the traditional skills of embroidery while praising quality British craftsmanship.

Workshops in a variety of embroidery techniques including Tambour beading, Silk Shading, Monogramming and Goldwork is taught throughout the year at the Hand & Lock Central London Atelier. The workshops cater to different skill levels allowing for both beginners and skilled embroideres to find a workshop suitable to their ability.

To discover Hand & Lock and the world of embroidery, head to www.handembroidery.com

Richard Saker

UNMADE is a start-up design company that has set out to 'revolutionise the fashion industry'. Working with the concept of 'fashion on demand', anyone can create one-off knitwear pieces by customising the patterns of a sweater or scarf using UNMADE'S clever interactive software.

Their impressive technical wizardry allows the customer to manipulate, using a touch screen, a realistic visualization of the sweater's patterns and colour to create their own variation of placement and scale, of any design. So far they have signed up fifteen designers with distinctive handwriting to create graphic patterns for customers to use, including Christopher Raeburn, Hiut Denim, and Katie Jones. It's a win-win scenario – each person has fun creating a custom design variation and UNMADE only produce goods that have been pre-ordered, so excessive production is avoided and satisfaction guaranteed.

The UNMADE knitwear brand is so called because each piece is unmade until the customer is involved; no stock is held. The sweaters are knitted in the standard manner using jacquard structures, either 'cut and sewn' or 'fully fashioned' (shaped pieces) in classic styles, made up on their premises and delivered next day with a personalized label.

Founded in 2013 by Ben Alun-Jones, Kirsty Emery and Hal Watts, who met at London's Royal College of Art, UNMADE'S blend of complementary expertise has led them to become an award-winning company. Ben is an interaction designer, skilled in digital visualization, and the brand's 'front man'. Kirsty is a fashion knitwear designer who has worked in Paris and London. She is now a hybrid of designer and technician and runs the in-house knitting machine. Hal, a former mechanical engineer, is the business brains of the trio. Their company has now grown to twenty-two people.

UNMADE has had pop-up stores, each complete with a knitting machine, in Covent Garden and Selfridges. More recent projects include a collaboration with Opening Ceremony and Farfetch.com. The speed of knitting technology – about 90 minutes per sweater – means that customers can see their piece being made, creating a direct link between owner/designer and manufacturing process. Others have previously attempted to create a knit-on-demand service, but UNMADE have realized the long-held dream of moving from mass production to mass customization, and now have their sights set on much larger collaborative projects with industry. A revolution indeed. ••• **Sandy Black www.unmade.com**

The embroidery on Hungarian textiles "wants to talk to you. And when you see the art that fills these clothes, you want to talk, too," explains Daniel Csonka of the Hungarian embassy in the Hague. The garments are "practical, of course. They are made to be worn. But they are also art." Daniel's first encounter with traditional Hungarian clothing came as a small boy during a school project. His father found him a wrangler's costume which included a Stetson-like cowboy hat. He remembers the pride he experienced as a young boy wearing that hat — and his surprise at how even the colours of the costume communicated something. "The different colours meant they came from different regions of Hungary."

From Sweden to Sardinia, the latest exhibition of the Textile Research Centre in Leiden, features over eighty examples of such pride and surprise. The material used ranges from goat's hair to satin, silk to flax, while the objects themselves include socks, chemises, shirts, dresses, belts and hats. **From Sweden to Sardinia: European Embroidery, until 27 February 2017 at The Textile Research Centre, Leiden www.trc-leiden.nl**

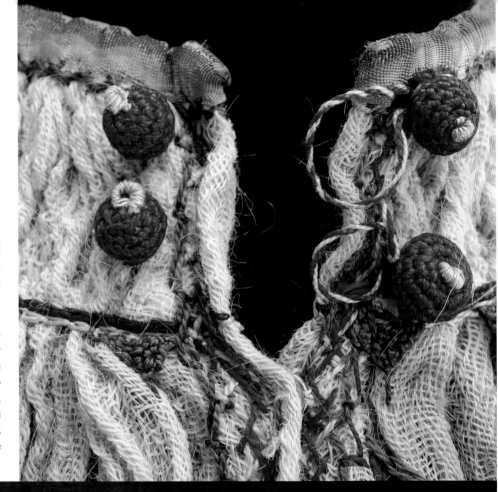

Unusually for an artist, Sidney Nolan was more recognised during his lifetime than after. Once considered one of the foremost international artists — he was particularly well known for his Ned Kelly series of paintings — he is now relatively little known. With 2017 marking the centenary of his birth, the Sidney Nolan Trust has developed a programme of events to celebrate the life and work of the Australian born artist once very much at the heart of the British art scene. Including Nolan's costumes for both the Royal Opera House and Royal Ballet, the exhibition at Pallant House Gallery promises to be a whirlwind of textiles, colour and movement. **19 February - 4 June, Transferences: Sidney Nolan in Britain, Pallant House Gallery, Chichester www.pallant.org.uk**

From bus seats to punch card systems *Weaving Futures* highlights the importance of woven textile design to the London Transport system, as well as the significance of the Jacquard loom. The project invites participants and visitors to consider the process of weaving cloth. Week by week a different artist or designer will be in residence at the Designology studio, working to a brief with a professional weaver who will interpret the maker's work into a digital woven textile prototype and ultimately on a state-of-the-art TC2 digital jacquard loom. With participants including Wallace Sewell, Eleanor Pritchard, and Gainsborough Silk Mill, responses to the brief are sure to span from future speculations on data capture and its textile use, to new methods of digitalising human interactions; and to creative interpretations and visualisations of existing TfL data sets. **Until 18 February 2017 London Transport Museum, Covent Garden Piazza, London WC2E 7BB www.ltmuseum.co.uk**

Traditionally the new year is focused around new beginnings, fresh approaches and personal resolutions. Whilst there is nothing new about our fondness for designers Kangan Arora and Kaffe Fassett, we can't help but be drawn to their latest ventures. Both designers have applied their fresh, colourful designs to bath and body collections. Kangan Arora's *Little Boxes of Joy* collaboration with REN cosmetics sees the luxury products and gift sets packaged in graphic patterns, as well as limited edition make-up bags. Prices range from £15 - £39. Kaffe Fassett has similarly applied his love of pattern and colour to his On Point collection, inspired by his geometric needlepoint designs. The range includes notes of bergamot, orange blossom and oleander – all exquisitely packaged in Kaffe's beautiful designs. Prices range from £8 - £22. **www.kaffefassettfragrance.com www.kanganarora.com/ren**

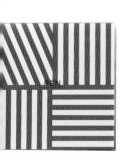

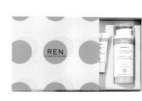
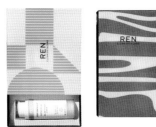

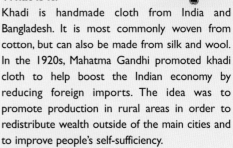

House of Cloth: Wool Khadi
What is it?
Khadi is handmade cloth from India and Bangladesh. It is most commonly woven from cotton, but can also be made from silk and wool. In the 1920s, Mahatma Gandhi promoted khadi cloth to help boost the Indian economy by reducing foreign imports. The idea was to promote production in rural areas in order to redistribute wealth outside of the main cities and to improve people's self-sufficiency.

How is it made?
Our wool khadi is made from pure sheep's wool. The wool is spun into yarn on a hand-cranked spinning wheel called a 'Charkha', before being woven on a handloom. These are narrow fabrics because they can only be woven as wide as an arm span.

Why we love it
The organic nature of the handmade wool inspires a sense of going back to basics, and any slubs, flecks and small knots in the weave add to the charm of the fabric. Because khadi is made by hand, the production does not require any fuel and produces little water waste, making khadi one of the most sustainable and eco-friendly fabrics available. By buying khadi we support local artisans and help maintain traditional production methods.

What is it used for?
Our wool khadi is thick and densely woven, making it a good insulator for cooler climates. As well as a beautiful fabric for coats, khadi wools are popular for scarves and blankets.

Wool, Cotton and Silk Khadi are all available from Cloth House, 47 Berwick Street, London, W1F 8SJ www.clothhouse.com

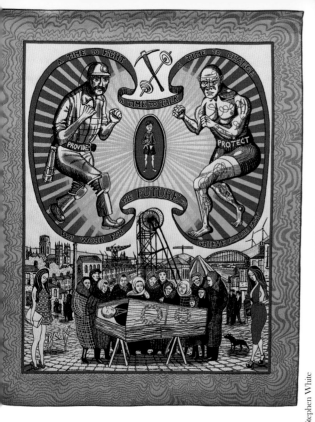

Grayson Perry's textiles star looks set to continue rising as his tapestry work is put on show at both *Collect: The International Art Fair for Contemporary Objects* and Durham Cathedral's exhibition *Textiles: Painting with the Needle*. Whilst Perry's *The Essex House Tapestries* will be on display alongside ceramics, glass, jewellery and textiles at Collect, his piece *Death of a Working Hero*, will hang next to textiles dating back 1,100 years. As ever the ceramicist/weaver/cultural commentator draws unexpected parallels through his work and display. **Collect: The International Art Fair for Contemporary Objects, 2 - 6 February, Saatchi Gallery, Duke of York's HQ, King's Road, London, SW3 4RY; Readers can claim two tickets for £28, plus one voucher for 50% off the show catalogue, quote SELVDJ17 www.collect17.org.uk, Textiles: Painting with the Needle, until 11 February, Open Treasure Collection Gallery, Durham Cathedral, Durham, DH1 3EH www.durhamcathedral.co.uk**

Pictured: Lisa Juntunen Roos. Photo by: Erik Thor

The textile masters and creatives of the future

Celebrating 135 years of Swedish craft education. Apply for our diploma and foundation courses in advanced textile craft and design.

For more information and application forms visit
Association of Friends of Handicraft:
www.hv-textil.se

Handarbetets Vänner Skola

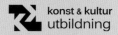

konst & kultur
utbildning

'The **course** has opened my eyes to ways of working in order to make a sustainable practice so that I can earn a living from what I **love**.' Ailish Henderson

 Open College of the Arts

LIVE | LEARN | CREATE

oca.ac.uk/sel

You can wear this as a slouchy beanie with the cuff turned down or as a little beret. It is quite a neat style so if you want to make it bigger you can increase it – by one horizontal repeat.

You will need: Jamieson's Shetland Spindrift yarn, One ball Natural White, main colour (MC), One ball Heron, contrasting colour (CC), 2.25mm circular needles 2.75mm circular needles. Tension: 32 sts, 42 rows = 10x10 cm

Finished Size: Circumference: 46cm, to be worn with up to 7cm negative ease Height: 23cm

Notes: You will knit in rounds on circular needles; for each round, read chart from right to left. When there is a long run between MC and CC, twist yarns every few stitches to ensure the long floats are secure and consistent knitting tension is maintained. A 24 stitch pattern chart and glossary is available from www.selvedge.org

Instructions: Using MC and smaller needles, cast on 144 sts. Work 9cm of K2, P2 rib. Change to larger needles. For the next round: K3, M1 ending with 192 sts. Join in CC. Following chart, repeat 24 stitch pattern 8 times across round, working decreases from round 27. Complete chart.

Finishing: Using a tapestry needle, sew end through remaining stitches and pull tight. Sew in any other ends and block over a form.•••

Hilary Grant: Knitting from the North: **Kyle Books, ISBN 978085783 3297** ~~£16.99~~ **£13.99 (incl. free P+P, UK mainland only) T: 01903 828503 and quote KB KN/SV or email mailorders@ lbsltd.co.uk**

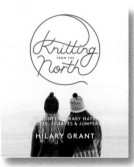

Make a tide beret from Hilary Grant's Knitting from the North

HYGGE *a heart-warming lesson from Denmark*

1 Royal brass wall sconse, 21cm, £265 www.theshopfloorproject.com 2 Felted Jannu Radhi Rug, 305 x 244cm, £785 www.stitchbystitch.eu 3 Huopaliike Lahtinen felt slipper, £52.95, www.selvedge.org 4 Small reduction fired tenmoku mug, £18, www.leachpottery.com 5 Alpaca Bed Socks, £15.50, www.jarbon.com 6 Gotland sheepskin rug, £395, www.toa.st 7 Wool cushion £150 www.margarethowell.co.uk 8 Frankincense, Cedar and Bergamot candle in a hand thrown pot by Marion Brandis, £35, www.asapoth.com 8 Tamar Mogendorff Mohair and Linen Bisons, 30cm, $80, www.tamarmogendorff.com

FIERCE AS FOLK

Charles Fréger's Wilder Mann

Photographer Charles Fréger's series 'Tribal Europe' captures contemporary incarnations of mythical folkloric characters from across the continent.

NIGHT BLOOMS

Fashion is suffering from a case of Tulip Fever

If summer florals suggest a sunny mood, winter florals cultivate a more mysterious mood; it's exotic, like the unexpected garden within the hold of a ship in Michael Ondaatje's novel *The Cat's Table*; sophisticated, like the Rockefeller grounds at Kykuit, designed to be visited at night as well as day; or magical, like Tim Walker's *Dress Lamp Tree, England* where the blossoming dresses glow amidst a twilight woodland. Indeed, Autumn/Winter 2016-17 offers a beguiling fashionscape of dark florals, lush night blooms that are carefully tended by their designers, and offered up in dramatic bouquets.

Erdem Moralioglu has so established his mastery of flowers – prints, appliqués, embroideries – that all his collections might be considered 'gardens of Erdem'. This season he looks to Old Hollywood, and to ingenues like Bette Davis and Lauren Bacall. His collection codes more 'floral fatale', however, with its shadowy film noir beauty: Barbara Stanwyck-blonde leaves and edgy white pistils climb the sleeves and kiss the hem of an ankle-length princess coat in mulberry tweed, or cling to the lapels of a peplum jacket cut from the same cloth. A floor-length gown fashioned from dotted black net, dove grey, and black glittering, appliqué flowers evokes the gleaming black and white of those early films, the potentially dangerous flowers beckoning a hapless hero toward them.

The flowers that adorn Dolce and Gabbana's collection look like they were plucked from the pages of a fairy tale. There is a rose-red inspired black evening coat trimmed in lush three-dimensional flowers in various sizes and shades of

rouge, a winning blend of fantasy and function. A striking print combining hydrangeas, colored daisies, poppies and appliquéd jewelled blossoms elevates a simple day dress with feminine details like a trumpet hem and dainty ruffled shoulders to suggest a strong heroine. And on a graceful black gown printed with oversized white tulips – hinting at the fairy tale kiss from 'two lips' that could awaken a princess or transform a frog into a prince – hot pink roses serve as power shoulders on a capelet that was shrugged over a top.

Zac Posen, on the other hand, takes his inspiration from a real-life princess – Elizabeth of Taro, the Ugandan royal – who was a lawyer, diplomat, model and, in 1969, the first black woman to grace the cover of Harper's Bazaar. The designer's colour palette of plum, burnt orange, purpled navy, fatigued moss and deep aqua, oversized Liberty prints all, brings a dark sweetness to the collection. Posen drapes the Liberty cotton as if it were a more luxurious fabric, fashioning elegant evening gowns fit for a princess. Most beautiful are his design details:

he gathers a pair of elbow-length sleeves into a blouson bodice; he tops a floor-length skirt with a handkerchief-hem capelet that sways gracefully down the catwalk. Posen's floral prints appear at once familiar yet exotic, in their magnified forms, fit for a royal who is also a professional woman.

Designer Paul Smith, in his "homage to the idea of the handsome woman", brings his menswear sensibility to a collection that puts women in tailored trousers, blazers and shirts. He cuts a pair of cigarette waist trousers from a hot-house floral, one that is almost cartoon both in proportion and mood, and pairs it with a trim button-up shirt in the same silk print. The juxtaposition of tailored, even severe, clothing with the exuberant print balances the two, softening the lines and adding an edge to the blooms. Smith chooses the same print with a glittery thread throughout for a day dress simply designed with a prim round neckline in front and a deep, open back. The shimmer highlights Smith's clean silhouette and suggests that the flowers are floating in a starry night sky.

In a collection largely populated by puffers, thick trench coats stretched off the shoulders and worn as dresses, oversized jean jackets and tweed suits rendered voluptuous by padded hips and shoulders, Balenciaga's florals provide a welcome respite in weight, if not in volume. These florals are strong and mismatched, pieced together in diagonal or vertical stripes that do not diminish the individuality of the prints. Asymmetry abounds, particularly in Balenciaga's 'high/low' or 'mullet' dress worn with peppermint-stick tights. The designer also shows ▶

Tim Walker

Zac Posen Autumn/ Winter 2016
Paul Smith Autumn/ Winter 2016
Balenciaga Autumn/ Winter 2016
Dolce & Gabbana Autumn/ Winter 2016
Comme des Garcons Autumn/ Winter 2016
Erdem Autumn/ Winter 2016

a floral ombre in orange, pink and yellow on a dark background: the pussy bow shirt with a shoulder flounce slowly gives way to a more bleached vision of the same print – right down to the toe of the knee-high boots. And a purple floral sheath revisits Balenciaga's signature pointy shoulders, a silhouette-sharpening move that adds an edge to an otherwise unconstructed dress.

Indeed Balenciaga's play with proportion and floral prints seems restrained when considering Comme des Garcons' vision of an eighteenth-century punk. Designer Rei Kawakubo stacks three tiers of floral 'hoop skirts' into a dress with padded velvet piping around the neckline, raw edges on each 'skirt'. And the technology peeks out from underneath the bottom layer: thick floral loops function as postmodern crinolines that support the volume of the fabric. Staged in Paris, Kawakubo's collection seems to conjure both a rebellious Marie Antoinette, via its untidy black court wigs and oversized pannier-inspired silhouettes, and a samurai, well cloaked in floral armour. Indeed, one black dress, covered in enormous quilted floral rings, might say, 'Let them eat bagels', while another looks like a protective series of shields attached to a corset.

These dark florals – flowers that come out at night, to be worn during the day – sidestep the sweet blossoms of summer and offer a mature vision that still can embrace play and whimsy. As represented in rich, sometimes moody palettes, these flowers have power; the woman who wears them this season will be no shrinking violet. •••
Kate Cavendish

International Festival of Fashion
and Photography at Hyères

Première Vision Prize
Céline Méteil
Ragne Kikas

Grand Jury Prize
Première Vision
Satu Maaranen
Kenta Matsushige
Annelie Schubert
Wataru Tominaga

CREATE, INSPIRE, SHARE.

#wearepremierevision

7-9 Feb. 2017
premierevision.com

PREMIÈREVISION
PARIS

YARNS / FABRICS / LEATHER / DESIGNS / ACCESSORIES / MANUFACTURING

ROYAL OPERATION

Inside the Wardrobe at the Royal Opera House

I'm in the basement of the Royal Opera House, Covent Garden looking at costume treasures. Here are the thirty-six snowflake tutus for *The Sleeping Beauty*, double-layered and decorated with elaborate detailing. There's the sweeping blue cloak worn by the mysterious magician Drosselmeyer in *The Nutcracker,* with its trick pockets for his magic tricks. I wander past rails of soldiers' tunics, dresses for garland girls and even a wolf outfit, where the tail neatly passes through a hole in the tights, allowing the dancer full body movement. It's a wonderful insight into the backstage life of The Royal Ballet.

The Royal Opera House is home to the largest collection of theatre costumes in the UK. Each year it lays on over fifty productions on its main stage alone. No wonder head of costume Fay Fullerton presides over a one hundred strong team (plus around sixty freelancers), with a department that extends over four floors of the building. With nearly everything – from props to dresses to wigs – made on site, the process involves long hours spent handcrafting each bespoke garment.

Costumes are made to last (some are still being used by the Royal Ballet forty years later). For each revival they are brought out of storage and fitted to the new cast in the workshops at the Opera House. Tailors work from the 'costume bible', that details original designs and subsequent revivals, to make sure that costumes stay accurate to their original design. Faded colours are re-dyed, worn darning is repaired. Working on five to six opera and ballet productions at a time, carrying out around 6,000 fittings per season, it pays to plan ahead. They buy in a small number of costumes for some contemporary productions: but where possible, if a show is not in use any more costumes are recycled for other shows.

Designing for live performance is different from designing for film because costumes have to be larger than life, so the audience can see them from any seat in the house. "Everything has to be more defined. with more depth to it. The colours also have to be stronger otherwise they just disappear on that stage," explains Fay. "Costume tells the story," she continues. "It develops the character, it plays a big part in the whole picture. But when performers go on stage they shouldn't be thinking about the costume. As it should become part of their body." Their most important job is to support the dancers. For ballet, the movement and lightness of the costumes is all important. For opera it's more about the singer being able to breathe naturally.

"Obviously the way period costume used to be made, they were a lot heavier than they are now," Fay explains. "Techniques and fabrics change over the years. Most ballet bodies have a small element of stretch in them even if it's velvet. Things have evolved quite quickly in terms of what we can do to make the dancers more comfortable." They can fake a heavy suit of armour or a bulky Tudor gown so it looks heavy. "With the older productions in the repertoire, if they can't find those fabrics anymore, we can copy them." The Opera House has "an amazing dye department where they do printing, hand-painting, everything you need to develop a fabric" and a digital printing machine that prints anything you want. "You just take a picture and you can recreate it on fabric, be it velvet, silk, cotton, chiffon."

Six months before opening night, costume fittings start for the chorus and the corps de ballet. Principals' fittings take place alongside rehearsals about six weeks before the first night. Once the costumes are made, they are then handed over to the 'running' team – who look after them for the duration of the shows, cleaning and preparing the costumes for each performance. The two big winter shows this year are *The Nutcracker* (with costumes designed by Julia Trevelyan Oman) and *The Sleeping Beauty* (with costumes inspired by Oliver Messel's original designs). The cast for *Sleeping Beauty* is huge; most wear three different costumes on stage, plus ballets have different casts on different nights. "We're talking about 400 costumes," says Fay dryly.

Fay studied fashion design and period costume at the London College of Fashion, then did a one year tailoring course. She joined the ROH as "the most junior costumier" in 1977, and worked her way up to her current post (she was appointed in 2013.) "I've worked in most areas of the Costume department, so I know how fabrics work, how they should be cut, what will work best for the dancers and singers – as soon as I look at a costume I know how much it will cost." Fay is the queen of historic period costume, but she and her team also get to work on radical new ballets ▶

by modern choreographers (she created the opulent costume designs for Will Tuckett's ballet, *Elizabeth*, earlier this year.) "We literally work on all periods here. You wouldn't just want to see big period pieces. You also want to see the future."

She's thrilled by the ROH's brand new state-of-the art Costume Centre which has just opened in Thurrock, Essex. Here the collection of over 20,000 costumes is kept in the very best climate-controlled conditions. There's a strong sense of history – the public can book tours of the collection and and take part in study days – but they're constantly thinking about training the next generation of designers. "The new building has a workroom for making chorus costumes for the stage here, and we've created an exciting new partnership with South Essex College to deliver a BA Hons degree in Costume Construction. Members of our team are involved in training and developing young talent for the industry."

In her spare time she goes to the National and the Old Vic, attends London Fashion Week and exhibitions at the V&A. "It is very important to know what's happening outside. I'm not sitting in a bubble at Covent Garden. International designers come in and work with us all the time, and I need to know all the techniques and ensure I am one step ahead, not one step behind." ••• **Liz Hoggard Backstage at The Royal Opera House: Join Selvedge for an exclusive tour of the Wardrobe Department, Thursday 9 March 2017 2.30-5pm www.selvedge.org**

Portrait Alun Callender, The Nose at Royal Opera House, Bill Cooper

RI- SING TALENT AWA- RDS

JAY
OSGERBY
SEBASTIAN
COX

TOM
DIXON
ZUZA
MENGHAM

SIR PAUL
SMITH
JOHN
BOOTH

ILSE
CRAWFORD
MARCIN
RUSAK

NIGEL
COATES
STUDIO
SWINE

ROSS
LOVEGROVE
GILES MILLER
STUDIO

SIX RENOWNED
DESIGNERS
NOMINATE

SIX RISING
TALENTS
FROM THE UK

With special thanks
to Sir John Sorrell
**SATURDAY
CLUB**TRUST

M&O PARIS
JAN. 20-24, 2017

PARIS NORD VILLEPINTE

THE LEADING DECORATION SHOW CONNECTING
THE INTERIOR DESIGN & LIFESTYLE COMMUNITY WORLDWIDE

MAISON
&OBJET
PARIS

#MO17 f 🐦 📷

WWW.MAISON-OBJET.COM

INFO@SAFISALONS.FR
SAFI ORGANISATION, A SUBSIDIARY OF ATELIERS D'ART DE FRANCE AND REED EXPOSITIONS FRANCE / TRADE ONLY / DESIGN © QUARTOPIANO - BE-POLES

FLORAL FREEDOMS

Printing the past and future

"Liberty is the chosen resort of the artistic shopper." – Oscar Wilde. Indeed Liberty must surely also be the resort of the artistic designer. With an ever-growing archive of designs dating from the 1880s to today, a consistently trend-setting fashion floor and an iconic arts and crafts setting, the textile design department at Liberty resembles no other.

Charged with the mission of combining the nostalgia of Tana Lawn with contemporary prints (and markets) is lead designer Polly Mason. Despite Liberty itself being a kind of beacon of heritage and design, it is nevertheless surprising to hear from Polly (who herself has had an unusually old school career trajectory, having worked in the print department at Liberty since only a week after graduating – nineteen years ago) just how traditional the design process is. The print department delivers two main collections a year – along with various other capsual projects – both of which begin life not as computer generated, digitally collaged mood boards but as drawings and gouache paintings, all done in-house. Furthermore Polly and her team go to great lengths to research before putting designs together. They have even been known to travel to Istanbul (for the Silk Road collection) and Ibiza (the Desert Island collection).

Whilst travel and gouache might be enough to inspire any designer, the "huge spectrum" of designs to refer to in the Liberty archive, along with surroundings akin to a contemporary fashion library, must surely be print paradise. •••
www.liberty.co.uk

PERENNIAL PRINTS

Josef Frank's Striking Botanicals

If you're visiting Stockholm for the first time and ask the locals where to go, chances are they'll send you to Svenskt Tenn, one of the must-see shops in the capital. For the Swedes, this legendary furnishings store is a source of national pride but, for the uninitiated, given Scandinavia's reputation for cool understatement, Svenskt Tenn may come as something of a shock. No minimalist abstracts here. Bold, high-voltage, colour-saturated florals are the order of the day, all created by one man, Josef Frank, up to eighty years ago.

Although Josef Frank is synonymous with Swedish design, he is also something of an anomaly. An Austrian émigré, he was born in 1885 and practised as an architect in Vienna until the age of forty-eight. It wasn't until 1933 that he moved to Sweden, fearing for his safety because of mounting anti-Semitism in neighbouring Germany following Hitler's rise to power.

Alongside his architectural work, Frank had also made a name for himself in Vienna as a furniture and textile designer, establishing a successful company *Haus und Garten* as an outlet for his talents in 1925. Design was pulling in different directions at this time, with the Bauhaus preaching the purist 'ornament is crime' dictum, while French artistes-décorateurs revelled in the joys of decoration. Josef Frank bridged these two idioms, designing pared down furniture and uncluttered interiors, enlivened by bursts of pattern in the form of colourful, dynamic block-printed textiles.

Having embarked on his career when Art Nouveau was all the rage, it was natural that Frank should be sympathetic to prevailing decorative trends. The Wiener Werkstätte, a powerhouse of Viennese pattern design established by architect Josef Hoffmann and artist Koloman Moser in 1903, was a formative influence on his aesthetic. The Wiener Werkstätte's dynamic block-printed dress and furnishing fabrics, produced from 1910 onwards, were refreshingly original and eclectic, with patterns ranging from punchy abstracts to zingy florals. Significantly, Josef Frank cut his teeth by selling textile designs to the Wiener Werkstätte, one of many artists and designers who fed into their collections.

In his furnishing fabrics for *Haus und Garten,* Frank's passion for botany resulted in designs that were strongly organic, both in structure and imagery. The long snaking stems that weave through his compositions were a device co-opted from William Morris, a designer he greatly admired. Another potent source of inspiration were the mille fleurs effects in French medieval tapestries, prompting a series of patterns with carpets of leaves and flowers evoking Alpine meadows.

When Frank moved to Sweden in 1933, his design vocabulary was already fully developed, so there was no radical change in style. In many respects there is a seamless continuity between his Austrian textiles of the late 1920s and his Swedish designs from the mid 1930s onwards. He even revived some of his earlier *Haus und Garten*

patterns, although in Sweden he chose the new medium of screen printing over block printing.

From an artistic and commercial point of view, Frank's success in Sweden was due to the tireless support of his patron Estrid Ericson, who championed and promoted his work through her company Svenskt Tenn. The name Svenskt Tenn, meaning Swedish pewter, alludes to the fact that metalwork was Ericson's primary interest when she originally established the business in 1924. However, within a few years Svenskt Tenn had expanded to encompass furniture and interiors. Having made contact with Josef Frank in 1932 when he was still in Austria, Ericson enlisted his services at Svenst Tenn following his arrival in Sweden. The partnership flourished and his friendship with Ericson remained as close as ever until his death in 1967, although he stopped designing textiles in 1950.

Picking up in Stockholm where he had left off in Vienna, Frank created appealing new mille fleurs patterns for Svenskt Tenn depicting Swedish wild flowers, such as 'Svenska Vårblommor'. Whereas his Austrian designs had been printed on white or buff cloth, he now began to experiment with black backgrounds, as in his famous pattern *Under Ekvatorn* ('Under the Equator'). To make the floral motifs stand out against this dark ground, he adopted a much brighter palette, including hot pinks and bluish purples. Another distinctive feature of Frank's oeuvre was the way he responded to specific habitats. During the Second World War, for example, he spent ▸

several years in the United States, prompting a series of patterns depicting North American flora and fauna. There is a decidedly exotic character to these designs, which include several *Tree of Life* patterns featuring fantastical trees with specimen fruit, flowers and leaves on their branches. Displaced from his familiar surroundings, Frank let his imagination roam free, abandoning plausible groupings and scientific accuracy in favour of a more liberated and fanciful approach to design. These patterns, although rooted in earlier textile traditions, were extremely avant-garde. The vividness of their compositions and their quasi-psychedelic colours prefigure the 1960s.

Frank's 'flower orgies' (as his patterns were characterised by Erik Zahle) triggered a wave of naturalistic florals in Sweden during the 1940s, including an appealing group of designs by Gocken Jobs for Jobs Handtryck. Even the Danish architect Arne Jacobsen fell under Frank's spell, creating a series of lush botanical patterns for Nordiska Kompaniet while exiled in Sweden during the war.

Describing this idiom as the 'Modern Florid style', Tyra Lundgren summed up the enduring appeal of Frank's textiles in the magazine Svenska Hem in 1943: "not only are they beautiful in colour and print but they also possess excellent quality as patterns per se. They have been composed with a rare knowledge of how patterns should be drawn in order to give an impression of imaginative wealth." It is this 'imaginative wealth' which gives Frank's designs such longevity. Although period pieces, his textiles still look incredibly fresh and still have the power to electrify contemporary interiors. ••• **Lesley Jackson**

JOSEF FRANK Patterns–Furniture– Painting 28 January – 7 May 83, Fashion and Textile Museum, Bermondsey Street, London SE1 3XF www.ftmlondon.org

HAND ME DOWN

Friends of Handicraft combine Tradition and Innovation

Friends of Handicraft, or Handarbetets vänner in Swedish, is an extraordinary textile institution with a rich and colourful history, intimately intertwined with the women's rights movement and the innovation of textile art in Sweden since the late nineteenth century.

Today, however, this combined textile studio and school is surprisingly little known among the general public. The historical building housing the institution is located in the beautiful Royal City Park Djurgården in Stockholm – the destination for Sunday walks and family picnics, and with popular neighbours like the Nordic Museum and Open Air museum Skansen – but until recently there were no signs whatsoever of the magic happening inside. Now, this is all about to change.

A couple of years ago former Swedish Fashion Council CEO Lotta Ahlvar was brought in with a brief to raise the profile and relevance of the institution in contemporary culture. One of her first measures was to reopen the ground floor gallery and to reintroduce a shop, offering textile materials – primarily for the students of Friends of Handicraft – but also literature, sewing kits and craft objects. The beautiful little gallery – with huge display windows facing the street – now lures in passers-by with a wide range of textile art related exhibitions, including anything from Friends of Handicraft exam students to Swedish and international textiles art luminaries.

"We are seeing a great resurgence of interest in textiles art today, for the first time since the hayday

in the 70s," Lotta Ahlvar says while showing me around the building. Apparently the somewhat odd height of the steps in the main staircase was once lowered to accommodate the floor-sweeping skirts of the ladies at the turn of the century. It is undeniably fascinating to imagine generation after generation of (mostly) women climbing these very stairs on their way either to the School of Friends of Handicraft or to the Studio.

Sophie Adlersparre, one of the three founding members of Friends of Handicraft in 1874, had a clear vision for the enterprise. In a time of rapid industrialisation and a blossoming national romantic movement, her aim was to establish an institution for the preservation of traditional peasant textile craft. An institution that would collect samples of

folklore textiles and also make sure that the age-old knowledge survived by making it relevant for contemporary life. Tradition and innovation, a dual ambition, is very much still in evidence today.

Friends of Handicraft was also innovative in that it was the very first financial venture in Sweden to be run entirely by women. Sophie Adlersparre was an avid women's rights activist and as the founder of the women's rights organisation Fredrika Bremerförbundet, as well as an editor of an important woman's magazine, she was an influential leader. At her side she had the artist and dress reform activist Hanna Winge, the first of many great artistic leaders that have pushed for creative and technical innovations while at the same time keeping traditions alive. During the golden years of Friends of Handicraft, in the mid twentieth century, the famous textile artist Edna Martin took the helm of the enterprise.

The Studio of Friends of Handicraft is currently one of Europe's few remaining studios for textile art and craft and the only one of its kind still in operation in the Nordic countries. The Studio employs six full-time weavers and needle workers (all women). The church and the military are the two main customers, keeping the studio busy with orders of ecclesiastical textiles and heraldic standards. When I visited, one of the master embroiderers was working on an impressive military standard. She told me that before it is ready and delivered, she will have spent about 1,500 hours working on it. On another stitching table a lavish gold needlework for the church is taking shape. One of the Studio's claims to fame is, by the way, a beautiful 1911 standard for the international woman suffrage alliance, still in use today.

Public artworks and collaborations with artists have always been of great importance to the institution and continue to be. Famous Swedish artists like Carl Larsson, Anders Zorn and Bruno Liljefors, at the turn of the century, then Siri Derkert, Karl-Axel Pehrson and Olle Baertling in the twentieth century and, today, Karin Mamma Andersson and Andreas Eriksson have all had their works realised by the skilled craftsmen at Friends of Handicraft. Some of the most famous grand-scale public textile art works produced by the Studio can be found in the Stockholm City Hall, the Swedish Parliament and the United Nations headquarters in New York.

The School of Friends of Handicraft was established in 1881 as a weaving school and is today housed on the floor below the Studio, with classroom after classroom filled with wooden looms from the nineteenth century – still in use. Offering both full-time programs and short courses in advanced textile handicraft and textile art, the three-year full time program boasts forty-eight students per year, and it is growing increasingly popular. "We have seen a steady increase in applicants in recent years," says Lotta. "And we have also been able to introduce a couple of new short courses this year, in shibori as well as silk shading and pearl embroidery." A promising sign it would seem, of the imminent comeback for textile arts and crafts. ••• **Susanna Strömquist www.hv-textil.se**

UNRAVELLING TRADITION

The Vocabulary of Carpets in Contemporary Art

Image Courtesy of Faig Ahmed Studio

In today's world, there aren't many great aesthetic traditions left to subvert. From pop-art to kitsch, and ever more rapidly in our post internet age, our perceptions, expectations, of traditional imagery have steadily altered. One might think that an artist seeking to rely on irony, defilement or unexpected uses of familiar forms would find the world's supply exhausted. Not so. A number of contemporary artists have found inspiration in a virgin medium – the Oriental carpet.

Oriental carpets are incarnations of the 'traditional'. They are prescriptive in design and the product of a continuous tradition; they are the antithesis of the contemporary. This contrast forms the central conceit of the installations created by the Azerbaijani artist Faig Ahmed. His work is characterised by a provocative relationship with formality, and traditional textiles are the foil to his rebellion. His pieces are recognisably Azerbaijani rugs, brightly coloured and geometrically-patterned. Yet their modernity slaps the viewer in the face. In the hands of Ahmed, carpets melt, bulge and distort. They exceed normal parameters and seep from the wall across the gallery floor. His use of pixilation and warping draws from op-art and digital internet aesthetics. One carpet liquefies *Oiling*, another pixelates *Tradition in Pixel*, and one, *Impossible Viscosity*, is rendered in melting tatters. The textiles give an impression of disfigurement. In his installation *Disconnected* the central threads of a stencil-like carpet are pulled out from the wall ▶

Stefan Altenburger, Courtesy the artist

and woven across the gallery space. The skeletal carpet has been eviscerated, and destruction forms an important aspect of Ahmed's inspiration. In a 2014 interview, he said of his work that it, "has given the carpet either new life or a total death because the old meaning was destroyed completely; but at the same time it's got a whole new meaning." It is tempting to side with 'total death'. To make one piece, *Recycled*, Ahmed sought out an old, rare Azerbaijani carpet. He turned it into a sculpture of the recycling symbol suspended above the remains of the ancient, beautiful carpet, in tatters on the floor beneath.

The way Ahmed draws inspiration from carpets may seem simplistic. It is not innovative to take what is visually familiar and subvert it by reconfiguring it into a psychedelic, seemingly digitised warp. Yet his work reflects an unresolved tension of our age. Crafts such as weaving rely on a vocabulary of image and design which is prescribed by tradition. In the case of contemporary art, however, originality is paramount and subversion praised. Ahmed has described finding himself a 'hostage to tradition', a situation he answered with aesthetic violence. Whether 'nothing perishes' in Ahmed's work, or if instead the death of tradition is the point, whether it represents destruction or deconstruction, carpets are the conceptual crux.

Decay, in an earthier way, is also the theme of the artist Martin Roth. He lays valuable carpets on the floor of an exhibition space, cultivating beneath them a grass lawn. The palimpsest effect is not unbeautiful, but each layer will eventually destroy the other. Ephemerality and transience are conveyed pretty poignantly, but once again it is difficult to shake the impression that the aesthetic achievement is rather pyrrhic. At best, Roth's work embraces the process of inevitable decay in a sensitive and poetic way. At worst, it is a desolate gimmick.

Rudolf Stingel has also exploited the visual potential of textiles. His 2013 installation at the Palazzo Grassi in Venice covered the walls and floors of the building in Oriental carpet. Stingler's installation is clever. It satisfies that key contemporary challenge: to alter the expected spatial relationship between artwork and viewer. Spreading over all interior surfaces, it produces an uncanny, enveloping, almost imprisoning aspect. Yet, similarly to Ahmed, Stingel's work is not about the textile itself in a conventional way. Neither the deep red colour nor the stylised geometric designs and their probable origin are a real concern of the work. Stingel in fact hung his paintings on the carpeted walls, rendering the textiles a backdrop. Yet when oriental carpets were first brought to Venice, from the Byzantine and later the Ottoman Empire, they were not regarded academically. They were decorative objects of luxury. When used to effect in a palazzo the impact of such carpets perhaps remains the same, even in the hands of Stingel. ▸

The visual appeal of carpets lies not only in the beauty and texture of their fabric, but also in their complex language of pattern. In Islamic countries carpet-making has long provided a means of non-representational artistic expression, resulting in a diverse repertoire of elegant, stylised motifs.

The oeuvre of Suzan Drummen draws inspiration from the sophisticated geometry of carpets, removing designs from their material context. She uses mirrors, glass and crystals, painstakingly laying them out over expanses of gallery floor in symmetrical patterns of roundels and medallions, not unlike the knots of a hand-woven carpet and paying tribute to the allure of rhythmic, curvilinear carpet design. Drummen is not the only contemporary artist to draw inspiration in a constructive way from the sophisticated patterns of Oriental carpets.

Jason Seife, based in Miami, makes modern carpets. His innovation is to do so in paint, modernising and altering their tone and colour. In his lifeless ink and acrylic copies of carpet designs, it is hard not to see superficial shadows of the subtle, luxurious and beautiful art of carpet-weaving.

Carpets may have given much to the world of contemporary art, in inspiration and actual material; but what contemporary trends will impart to the weaving tradition remains to be seen. ••• **Cosima Stewart**

Right: Robert Fontaine Gallery. Opposite: Hugo Rompa

ALPINE INSPIRATION

Moncler's subversive yet traditional collection

Well, the British Winter has been in full swing for several months now and it is the season of layers; cardies, gloves, scarves, jackets, overcoats, big tote bags to carry extras, and general bundled up-ness. Alternatives to the 'walking wardrobe' chill deflection method do exist though, and one to adopt is a lightweight but costly down-filled jacket, or coat option – but the stylishness of these often lumpy overdoings can be somewhat variable. However, since 1952 when Rene Ramillon founded his specialised down-plumped and warm as toast, mountain climbing wear company, Moncler has become the go-to brand for top of the range, luxurious and damnably fashionable duvet dressing. Created as an abbreviation of 'Monestier-de Clermont' a picturesque French Alpine town, the brand name Moncler is now synonymous with luxury high fashion for both indoors and outdoors, All these years later it has returned to its Alpine source to inspire the 2016/17 Autumn/Winter 'Gamme Rouge' collection.

Designed by Giambattista Valli, this collection brings together and realises a whole heap of ideas from Alpine and Tyrolean traditional dress, as well as Swiss, Hungarian and Ukrainian Folk embroidery. Setting the scene, quite literally, is a simple, classic down coat with a deep, deep white fur hem depicting a typically snow-capped, digitally printed Alpine view. Balancing the full-bodied fur the garment's surface is heavily textured with tightly packed embroidered flower motifs of a beautiful, elemental hue. Glinting from between the riot of flower heads peek little spangly, crystal renditions of snowflakes.

Fur, especially the winter white variety, features large in this collection and is even, rather bizzarely fashioned into a pair of hotpant style lederhosen, complete with a set of Hungarian influenced red embroidered harness braces. Although these beauties indeed offer the promise of a satisfyingly cosy lower middle to upper lower area, there are other, significant bits of personage left out to chill, especially if worn with the wisps that Giambattista Valli sees fit to team them with. Valli's vision of partnership for these fuzzy trunks is a Tyrolean inspired, delicate, white on white embroidered translucent organza blouse, which to be fair is fitted with a chunky knitted rollneck. Valli has come up with more wearable apres ski options: a similar, gorgeous blouse with white Swiss style embroidery on black organza, matched with a micro dirndl skirt in the same fabric, plus lederhosen harness braces, potentially in the red patent leather version – oh, and elevated wooden clogs.

Of course, Moncler is situated in high fashion land so many designs, ideas and items in the collection are great fun and individually might even be absorbed into the wardrobes of non-Klosters folk. There are also really useful yet glamorous pieces that could just cheer up a squally grey winter's day. To chase away the chills, crimson cross stitch embroidery, a staple of traditional Ukranian folk decoration, appears on the polar-hued panels of cuddly but tailored down jackets, and also makes its way into oversized, puffy yarned intarsia knits. To add sparkle and light to dark days, and as a further nod to traditional knits, the snowflake motif (so often seen in Nordic and Fairisle designs) appears in the guise of a jewel put together from semi precious stones and bugle beads. Placed on sleeves, shoulders, single and in multiples, these little pieces of luminescence are the insignia of those who are determined to make the most of all weathers.

There are also quieter, arguably more elegant moments in this collection provided by the clotted cream coloured, baby-lamb soft bouclé pieces trimmed with fur collars, hems and cuffs. If fur is not for you (or me) then quite understandably Moncler as a brand, and this collection in particular, might be tricky to appreciate. However, there are other, textile only pieces to enjoy, such as a truly lovely coat, which is almost alive with complex surface enrichment. Blue flower motifs shower a ground of layered Richelieu embroidery: the daisy appliqué makes a further spike-petalled appearance and mini jewelled snowflakes dot the surface of this extraordinary garment.

Notwithstanding some lack of practicality and what is for some a controversial use of fur, Valli's real success with this collection is that he has brought some very beautiful and meaningful aspects of traditional textile culture into high end fashion and made it work. Often embroideries and patterns fail to move beyond 'folksy-ness' and as a result indicate only a Bohemian, or homespun interpretation – which is fine but it is good to see alternatives to that too. This collection, with its array of influences, demonstrates that the Folk textiles, which are repositories of narrative, heritage and tradition can be contemporary, edgy and sexy as well as comfortable and warm. ••• **Nicola Donovan**

COLD COMFORT

Keeping warm in Siberia

It covers eight time zones, stretches from the Ural Mountains in Western Russia to the Pacific coast in the Far East and takes about seven hours to fly across in a jet. Siberia is vast. From the air, much of the northern part of Siberia looks like a wilderness, seemingly endless forest and tundra interspersed by the occasional river, road, town or village. It may appear empty from the air, but it's home to at least nineteen different groups of indigenous peoples. Some of these cultures have existed there for a thousand years or more. In the Soviet era they were often referred to as the 'Small Peoples', the name having more to do with their population than stature. Today, the smallest group are the Entsy, who number just 227 people, while the largest group is the Nenets who have a population of over 44,000.

The primary activity of most of these northern Siberian peoples is reindeer breeding, along with hunting, trapping & fishing. It is fur from the reindeer they breed and the animals they hunt and trap, that provides them with the materials they need for making their traditional clothes. Siberia can be bitterly cold during the winter months when temperatures can plummet below -60°C, but native people cope with this by using fur for their winter clothes. Reindeer skin is used by peoples around the Arctic to make coats, parkas, trousers, boots, hats and mittens, as well as bags and household items. It is remarkably durable, as well as being windproof and water repellent. It also offers the best insulation against the cold and is much more effective than goose down or man-made fibres. The reason for this is that reindeer have a thick under fur close to their skin which traps air; and also, reindeer hairs are hollow which gives excellent insulation against even the severe cold of a Siberian winter. Most reindeer skin clothing is made from summer hides as the hair is shorter, making it less bulky.

Making skin clothing is a lengthy process and there is a huge amount of work involved in preparing a reindeer skin for sewing. It has to be cleaned and any trace of fat or meat removed. The leather is then worked on using scrapers and other tools until it reaches a stage of softness that can be sewn easily. For items of clothing where just the ▶

leather is used, the hair has to be cut off, and the skin may also be dyed.

The Chukchi people from the North East of Siberia often use alder bark to dye reindeer leather as they like the rich dark tan colour it gives, while Northern peoples use a variety of natural dyes for both their skin and fabric clothes. They obtain these dyes from a range of different trees and plants that include aspen, alder, larch, wild rosemary, tinder fungus, fire weed and blackberry. The colours used in traditional clothing tend to be a combination of cultural tradition and personal preference. The Khanty people in Northwest Siberia like to use the colour red. This preference is based on their traditional belief, that red represents the middle world, the current world in which they live. White is the colour of the upper world which is inhabited by good spirits while black represents the lower world of the dead and bad spirits. The Nenets like to wear bright colours for their fabric dress and also on the trim of their fur clothing. This probably originates from the traditional Nenets belief that 'Num', their principal deity, dresses himself in a rainbow.

The actual design of northern peoples' traditional clothing varies from region to region considerably. Some of the clothes are quite plain, others are more complex with designs that incorporate beadwork, dyed fabric, and metal ornaments. Above all, the clothes are practical, comfortable and suit both the local climatic conditions and the lifestyle of the people. Reindeer herding is an active occupation and the Nenets man's 'Malitsa' is an ideal design for this. It's basically a hooded knee length tunic, made of reindeer skin, which is gathered and belted at the waist. It allows the wearer considerable freedom of movement, while also keeping them warm. When worn in conjunction with their traditional thigh length reindeer skin boots (pimy), it offers good protection from the extreme cold of a Siberian winter. The malitsa also has reindeer skin mitts sewn on to the bottom of the sleeves, so finding your mittens is never a problem!

One of the more unusual items of women's traditional clothing is the 'Kerker' which is worn by Chukchi women of Chukotka in the far ▶

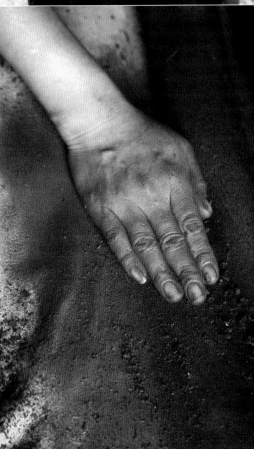

north east of Siberia. It's a kind of very loose fitting onesie, an overall made from young reindeer hides. It reaches down to the knees, with a deep plunging neckline, loose trousers, wide sleeves and a fur collar. It is normally worn together with high fur boots (torbases). The summer Kerker is made from a single layer of skin with the fur worn inside, while the winter version has a double layer for extra insulation and warmth.

To the west of Chukotka, on the Taymyr Peninsula, live the Nganasan people who also wear distinctive clothing. Women there wear reindeer skin overalls together with a parka usually made of white reindeer and a bonnet-like white reindeer skin hat. Both men's and women's outer clothing are decorated with fabric, mostly white, red and black broadcloth, which is used mainly as trim. The clothes are decorated with detailed appliqués or geometric patterns which indicate their owner's social standing, what area, and clan they were from, as well as their marital status. Perhaps the most remarkable aspect of Nganasan clothing is the design of their white reindeer skin boots (faimu) which are cylindrical and don't narrow at the ankle.

My favourite item of all traditional northern Siberian clothing is the Nenets women's Yagushka. The Yagushka is an ankle length coat made with a double layer or reindeer skin usually with a collar of white arctic fox fur. The inside of the coat has the fur facing inwards while the outside has the fur facing outwards. The coat opens down the front, is fastened by a series of leather straps and held closed by a belt made from woven coloured wool with a large copper or brass buckle. What makes the Yagushka so special is its decoration. It has beautiful traditional patterns which are made from inlaid pieces of light and dark reindeer fur, often edged with coloured cloth. They can look spectacular and making a Yagushka can take many months.

All Nenets women from reindeer herding families are taught to sew from childhood. By the time they become adults, every woman will have their own traditional reindeer skin sewing bag with a needle case and a small thimble bag fastened to it. ••• **Bryan Alexander**

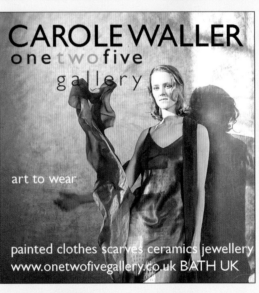

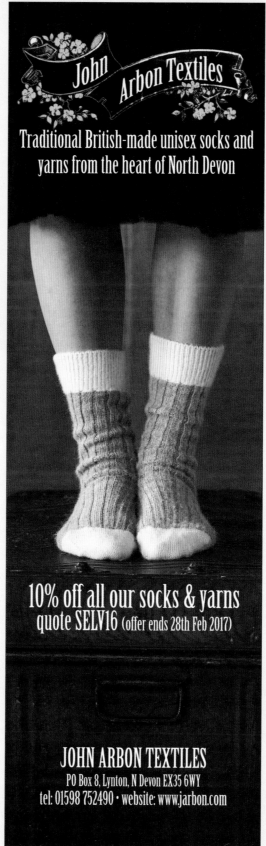
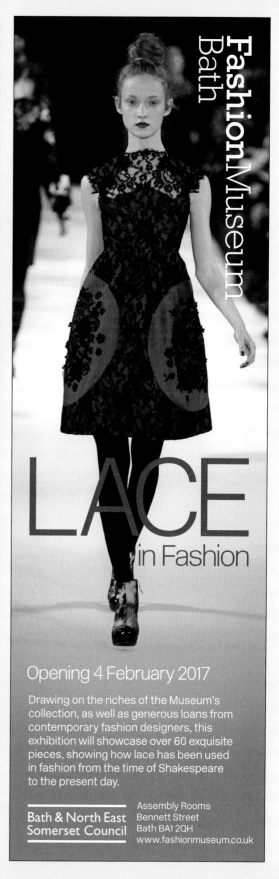

ACTING THE GOAT

Vedat Demiralp is shepherding the revival of Turkish rugs

Memories from his childhood in the Black Sea region came flooding back when Vedat Demiralp spied a remarkable rug on a friend's floor whilst visiting Turkey twelve years ago. He was reminded of the special rugs woven from goat hair which were, at one time, an honoured part of a woman's dowry. Highly valued and painstakingly handmade, these deceptively simple rugs were considered an important part of Turkish rural culture.

As Turkey's rural population has migrated away from remote mountainous areas to the cities in search of work, these rugs have almost entirely disappeared. Younger generations are drawn towards the colourful, mass production of the late twentieth century and these monochromatic rugs have become casualties of such trends. Demiralp visited the village where they were still being made and sold. In the past these rugs would have been made on a regular basis, at home, to supplement a family's income; but as demand has declined so too have the skills required. He found the weavers in their forties and fifties, and not all of the designs good – but there were some lovely examples. Since then he has founded Coban Rugs and dedicated himself to reviving and refining the designs and reintroducing the skills. He began hiring the best weavers to make them for him and his predominantly UK based, interior design market. While remaining completely loyal to the original concept he has fine-tuned their production.

Exquisitely plaited edges adorn and finish the rugs; delicate and abstract motifs travel lightly across the surface. These are often hand stitched by Demiralp himself after the rug has been woven and are also inspired by his other loves – technology and engineering. Linear rhythms of geometric shape in contrast with the natural tones of the fibres come together, giving them a striking appearance. Their palette is highly specific and results from the natural colour of the goat's hair. Demiralp explains that the goat hair is naturally resistant to dye; a high level of lanolin makes it hard to apply any colour. The goat's natural habitat is invariably mountainous and they can survive in most climates; high altitudes, hot, dry summers and cold, crisp winters. The resulting goat hair is varied and contains several different types of hair. The most (famously) desirable is the soft hair found under their chins and bellies, cashmere. But they also have a very coarse hair which runs along their spines and several other grades in-between.

The key to production here is the shepherd. In fact "çoban" means "shepherd" in Turkish and the whole process starts with buying the hair, at the right time from the best shepherds. Usually shorn in spring before the hot weather sets in, the goat hair is removed (with no harm to the goat I'm assured) in one fell swoop, which means all the different types of hair are mixed together. In some ways, Demiralp explains, the 'combing' process is the most important part, as this is where the different colours and grades of hair are separated out. The combing is done in several stages. As the hair travels through a combing machine the impurities are removed, along with a quarter of the hair which is unusable and impossible to spin. At each stage the comb gauge becomes finer and the quality of hair becomes thinner. After this process the hair is spun, an extremely time-consuming process – it takes a spinner two to three days to create enough fibre for one day's worth of weaving.

Unlike wool, goat hair is complex and difficult to work and the person spinning must be a real master of their craft. It's something they can only learn by touch and 'feel', according to Demiralp: certain weavers can only work with thread spun by certain spinners as they get used to a particular quality of fibre. If he pairs up different and new weavers and spinners together they can take several days longer to create the rug if they are unfamiliar with each other.

Despite struggling to find young people to train he has gradually created a successful flow of production and now offers an exclusively bespoke service. Production times can vary from three weeks to three months depending on the time of year and complexity of the rug. The final stage of production is the finishing. Generally they are woven in sixty to seventy centimeters widths which is suitable for a stair runner: if a floor rug is required the strips will be woven up to one metre wide and stitched together to create a larger size, with any embellishment or fringing added by hand at the very end. Demiralp concludes that, for now, he has contributed significantly to revive the tradition; its minimal, yet highly crafted, aesthetic proves popular in the UK. His aim is to explore the over-stitching technique further and elaborate their two-dimensional motifs – perhaps even adding a tiny touch of colour, he says with a laugh. •••
Ptolemy Mann www.cobanrugs.com

Aiguille en Fête
Paris

The French event for
textile arts and crafts lovers

From February 2nd to 5th 2017

Paris - Porte de Versailles

240 exhibitors - 40 000 visitors

2017 theme

SCANDINAVIAN MOOD

Exhibitions - Workshops - Events Free!

QuiltSewingTraditionsKnittingEmbroideryHaberdasheryLaceDream

Buy your tickets on :

www.aiguille-en-fete.paris

With

MODES
&TRAVAUX

THE GOSPEL TRUTH

Ethel Mairet Picking up the Threads of Tradition

Delving into the collection of Ethel Mairet's hand woven and naturally dyed textiles at Ditchling Museum of Art & Craft is like rummaging through a brand new sweet tin at Christmas. They are a feast of potent colour combinations and sublime textures, and guaranteed to quietly thrill the most discerning creative eye.

This collection dates from the 1920s when Mairet, inspired by the developing artistic community in the village, moved with her second husband Philip Mairet to Ditchling to live and work at Gospels their newly built Arts & Crafts home and workshop. Whilst few of her garments remain intact in museum collections, her weaving sample portfolios used in teaching, are abundant. A few are annotated with Mairet's instantly recognisable handwriting, but most remain without description.

The museum is also home to Mairet's photograph album from the 1930s which is filled with images of her students working at Gospels: a cheerful plaid jacket; two jaunty tam o' shanters made from offcuts; a large zipped terracotta pocket, and, intriguingly, a matching rescued biased hem. And there is a beige and brown silk scarf recently acquired with a romantic story attached. It is from a woman whose parents exchanged Mairet scarves shortly before their wedding in the 1930s and there is a lovely photograph showing the couple in their winter coats and matching scarves. These have recently gone on loan to Mashiko Museum of Ceramic Art near Tokyo, Japan, as part of their new exhibition *Enchanted with Ethel Mairet* which pays homage to her influence in their craft town, and where her seminal treatise *Book on Vegetable Dyes*, written a century ago, is still used today by ninth generation weaver and dyer, Mr Tadeshi Higeta.

Ditchling Museum of Art & Craft is also celebrating the centenary of this book with an exhibition entitled *Dyeing Now: Contemporary Makers Celebrate Ethel Mairet's Legacy* in which contemporary textile designers and dyers are invited to recreate Mairet's one hundred dye ▸

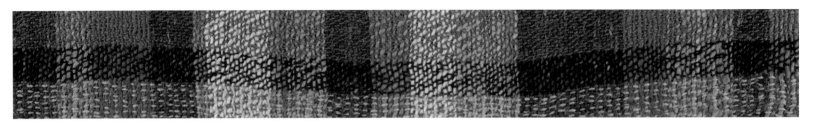

recipes and show their work alongside the museum's collection. Mr Higeta's work will also feature in the display.

Mairet's place within the Arts & Crafts movement in Britain during the early twentieth century is assured. She and her first husband Ananda Coomaraswamy, an Anglo-Ceylonese geologist and six years her junior, began their unconventional marriage in 1902 travelling to Ceylon (now Sri Lanka) on his mineralogical survey. They certainly shared an interest in the traditional crafts.

Mairet began to amass indigenous textiles. She taught embroidery, and contributed extensively to Ananda Coomaraswamy's seminal work *Medieval Sinhalese Art* with her own research and photographs. Their return to England, and perhaps their subsequent marriage breakdown, galvanised Mairet into action, and by 1910 she had acquired a loom. She was close friends with C R Ashbee, architect, designer and founder of the Guild of Handicraft, and his wife Janet, writing to them on her travels and updating them of her progress in learning to weave and dye yarn and cloth.

Mairet's move to Ditchling consolidated all that she had worked towards, and her belief in the future of craft was encapsulated in *An Essay on Crafts and Obedience* (1918) written with Philip. Conscious of her lack of a formal training, and the impossibility of acquiring an authentic craft apprenticeship as followed by the guild tradition, she encouraged practitioners to learn from all available resources, picking up the broken threads of tradition from everywhere as individuals. She shared a common view with many of her Ditchling contemporaries that the sustainability of craft lay in the teaching of a new generation of students.

To that end she set up her own courses at Gospels, and taught at Brighton School of Art. She employed apprentices and trained girls from the village to spin, make warps and throw a shuttle. The weaving workshop and dyeing shed were always dynamic and alive

TO·THE·WEAVING·ROOM

with experimentation. If all this sounds a haven of keen hobbyist amateurism, the evidence points in the other direction. Mairet was not interested in satisfying the creative needs of the middle class homemaker, and indeed the success of Gospels was very much down to her commitment to a set of values and standards, as well as her ambition.

In 1930, she found herself alone again – her joint venture with Philip at The New Handworkers Gallery in London ended, as did their marriage; he had taken up with a colleague. During that time Mairet took on students from around Europe, some of whom had been trained in industry and were technically more proficient than she was.

Their expertise and differing influences revolutionised the work produced at Gospels: the textiles which had hitherto been a simple relationship between colour and texture expressed in plain weaves gave birth to more complex weave designs, through more sophisticated and extensive colour and yarn combinations. The fabrics left the workshop with a Gospels label; this democratised the work but we are left unclear as to who specifically designed and made each piece.

Mairet was not keen on having men in the workshop, but on rare occasions she made an exception. One was Valentine KilBride, a young man from Bradford who had been taught weaving and dyeing for industry and was disillusioned with mass production. In the museum's collection is a wonderful thick silk flapper dress woven by KilBride for Mairet, jaunty and red with fringes and tassels hanging from the shoulders. It is hard to imagine it on Mairet, the suffragette supporter, and radical dress reformer – but perhaps it is evidence of a lighter, more playful and dramatic side.

By the 1940s and until her death in 1952, the Gospels workshop was established in Britain. Mairet's commitment to hand weaving and natural dyeing being inspirational, and giving a creative lead to industry, paid off and she was the first woman to be awarded Royal Designer for Industry. She exhibited widely with the Arts and Crafts Exhibition Society, the Little Gallery, the Three Shields Gallery, and the Red Rose Guild exhibitions alongside her contemporaries – textile designers Barron and Larcher, and potters Bernard Leach and Michael Cardew. From 1934 to 1951 she sold her work at her own shop in East Street, Brighton.

In recent times, Britain has undergone yet another craft revival, a response to an evergrowing technological age in which we feel more and more removed from the physical act of making. Once again we are seeing a renewed interest in Mairet and her work by a new generation of makers, engaging with traditional crafts in their new live/work units in a bid to revive a more human scale, environmentally friendly and ethical combination of living and working.

Mairet's commitment to learning from craft traditions, using them to fit the context of today in order to sustain them for the future, is very much at the heart of the exhibition at Ditchling Museum of Art & Craft. The museum will be amassing works dyed specifically for the exhibition over the course of the display, and in that fashion it will grow organically and help to establish those working today in Mairet's footsteps to keep craft alive for future generations. ••• **Donna Steele**
Dyeing Now: Contemporary Makers Celebrate Ethel Mairet's Legacy, until 16 April, Ethel Mairet Living Legacy: natural dyeing and weaving masterclass 3-7 April www.selvedge.org, Ditchling Museum of Art + Craft, Lodge Hill Lane, Ditchling, East Sussex, BN6 8SP. www.ditchlingmuseumartcraft.org.uk

HANDSPUN

Thibault Van Der Straete spins a good yarn

It was a love of alpaca that took the French fashion designer Thibault Van Der Straete to Peru. In the early 1990s, he scoured the markets for blankets and vintage ponchos, gradually building mutual trust with local vendors in Lima and Cuzco. By 2008 he had moved permanently to Lima where he runs his company today. His alpaca collections include machine-knitted sweaters, hand-woven blankets and vintage ponchos that he artfully transforms into home decoration.

"Traditional craftsmanship in Peru is slowly disappearing. It's not profitable enough so the young generations have turned to the gold mining industry," he sadly admits. However his early passion for hand-spun and hand-woven alpaca remains intact. Deeply committed to preserving ancient crafts and maintaining social cohesion, he's about to purchase a house in the Sierra to set up a sustainable weaving community – a place where young people could stay for several months, make a living, learn hand skills from their elders and perpetuate Peruvian textile crafts. "There are very few spinners left, and hand-spun alpaca yarn has become rare.

When the Civil War erupted in the early 1980s, the people of the Sierra fled their villages and resettled in Lima. Their children cannot speak Quechua but they speak English fluently and don't care much about traditional textiles. I've been working with the same based Serranos woman and her extended family for the past twenty five years. They manufacture my sweater collections; 12,000 pieces a year and help me maintain the production of hand-woven blankets in the Peruvian Mountains. The Quechua people spin and weave during the rainy season and work in the fields from April to September. Typically, a blanket requires seven to ten days of hand spinning and is then woven by hand in three days. I wouldn't be able to produce hand-crafted blankets in the Sierra without the help of this Quechua family. We work very closely together."

With the overall industrialisation of alpaca fibre, the majority of Andean farmers sell their raw fleece to the local cooperatives that are the main suppliers of the Peruvian yarn manufacturers: "Raw alpaca has become so scarce in the Sierra and so valuable to me that I don't dare to dye it anymore. Natural alpaca is a beautiful and special fibre, with up to twenty five different colours that range from white to black with infinite shades of greys, fawns and browns. You can't be too picky about colours nowadays; it all boils down to locating the rare material at the Sierra's weekend markets, and buying whatever colours you can find, wherever you can find it. It can take a full year to find a specific brown. Sometimes alpaca raw fleece is purchased 300km away from where the spinners and weavers live and in the harsh environment of the Sierra, the delivery is not an easy task." •••
Anne Laure Camilleri www.selvedge.org

SHOP TALK NO 3

Jane Audas shopping at The Shop Floor Project

This series of Shop Talk articles has been about shops you can walk into and experience the tactile pleasure of objects and the tacit pleasure of knowledgeable customer service. The other retail to appreciate is the visual, laid-back browsing experience of a great website. The Shop Floor Project website is run by mother and daughter Denise and Samantha Allan. Both are fine artists by training, and it shows in how their site looks and in the products they sell. The site isn't your usual e-commerce offer. You can't, for instance, filter stock by price. Instead they give us stories about makers, stories behind objects and then they photograph the objects in a suggestive manner, encouraging a 'click to add to basket' before you know it.

The Allans are based in scenic Cumbria: with an online business you can live somewhere very pretty indeed and sell the world over. They describe what they do with Shop Floor as 'curating, designing and co-curating'. The site began because they were both interested in how things were made and sourced. It was called The Shop Floor Project as at first they didn't quite know how to define what they were hoping to do: hence 'on the shop floor' and 'project' as it allowed them time to form their selling practice. The stock selection is quirky and unapologetic too. It includes waxed cotton fisherman's coats and armorial cutlery by Japanese designer Mitsuhiro Konishi; hand-woven baskets made by the women of the Tuareg, a nomadic African tribe; graphic Scottish lambswool blankets and painterly cushions featuring naive collages of writer's houses by Amanda White; as well as other treasures. The site changes as stock comes and goes. Some products, however, are recurring, like sconces and chandeliers by Malin Appelgren and bird ceramics by Michaela Gall. Increasingly the Allans are designing and co-designing the products they sell, and have an adjacent business designing products for museums, which Samantha knows well from a previous work life. They have just designed new scarves inspired by ancient Greek and Roman glass in the British Museum. The names of the scarf colourways alone make them covetable – clay, plaster pink and rust.

Product development takes anything from months to years but it is without a doubt worth the wait. The new animal paintings from cult Japanese artist Miroco Machiko were a long time coming – but how grand and dramatic they are. Pleasingly, they have smaller Miroco Machiko animal calendars for those of us saving up for a painting. Andrea Shemilt Kashanipour's candlesticks are inspired by 19th century Staffordshire figures and they are joyous enough to perk up any mantelpiece. And Japanese maker Yukihiro Akama's wooden houses, carved in Yorkshire, epitomise the unusual combinations present in many of the Shop Floor's projects.

The Allans have just celebrated their ten year anniversary running Shop Floor. That is a long life in Internet years. So many 'lifestyle' websites come and go. Mind you, 'lifestyle' is a grim word, reducing the things we live with to something here today, replaced tomorrow. A life lived with style is a different thing and is something The Shop Floor Project site can certainly help you with. •••
www.theshopfloorproject.com

PERMANENT COLLECTION

The philosophy behind the Korean label Oma

"An object in a museum case… must suffer the denatured existence of an animal in the zoo," observes Bruce Chatwin's narrator in his novella *Utz*. "In any museum the object dies – of suffocation and the public gaze – whereas private ownership confers on the owner the right and the need to touch." Chatwin's *Utz* is speaking of porcelain, but he voices a sentiment that regularly troubles the revival of traditional craft skills. Museums archive examples but keeping skills and knowledge alive – rather than offering custodianship of objects – is a different challenge entirely.

"I started to think about precious things," explains the Korean designer Oma when I enquire about the origins of her eponymous design label. Based in Seoul, Oma now spends several months of each year overseeing hand production in the picturesque region of Chiang Mai in northern Thailand. The launch of her first clothing collection in 2010 at the celebrated Livingstone Studio in Hampstead was prompted by her sense that traditional textile production methods in Korea were dying out. "I was ashamed to see ancient textile practices disappearing," she explains; hand crafted textiles were visible "only in a museum or gallery – but not really alive."

Oma's approach offers us an antidote to fast fashion, although she is quick to correct the assumption that fashion alone is the culprit. "It is not fashion and textiles only. All consumption is going so fast," she reminds me, referring to our "speed obsessed environment". Fast fashion is sold to us as an expansion of choice. Don't like what you see this week? Come back next week: colours, hemlines and cuts will have changed. Bored with your look? Minimal investment can correct it all: bin everything and start again! Oma doesn't subscribe to this logic, instead seeing that "mass production potentially narrows choice." We may now be awash with volume, but as consumers we do not enjoy much variety of choice. In response to this quandary, Oma set about sourcing textiles made by hand that could become the basis of the collections she designs. "We work by hand as much as we can – it has different energy – a human spirit."

Admittedly, it is a business approach fraught with challenges. "There are very few artisans left in Korea," she explains. A technical rather than hands-on education is popular throughout the region and traditional techniques do not – at least for now – interest many emerging Korean designers. (Oma's own textile education in Korea focused on technology and she admits her interest as a student in studying natural dye recipes from the elderly women still practising was hardly a popular course of action at the time.) Today her inspiration continues to come from "an artisan's way of working". She sees the steps to textile production by hand such as spinning or weaving as "processes that are spiritual" and cites the Indian textile design company Raag as a model of inspiration, again taking the local but working with a sophisticated contemporary eye. ▸

Two years ago Oma began work with artisans in northern Thailand, specifically weavers who plant the very cotton they later spin and weave into cloth. Here too traditional skills are disappearing, although her diagnosis is that rather than lacking in skill, Thai artisans are hampered by a lack of design development. "The skill is great, but the design is not. In Thailand now, traditional skills are disappearing because the design is too ethnic." She has found Thai artisans "more open minded" and receptive to change than her efforts to work with Korean artisans who, she concedes with a chuckle, "sometimes keep doing things their way and just don't want to change."

For a designer (with experience in London at Alexander McQueen's studio prior to the start of her company) this business model offers great potential. Oma needs skilled artisans to execute her designs – garments which nod to their Asian roots but are a far cry from out-dated tourist craft. She describes her collections as sharing an "uncomplicated garment line" before clarifying that she "does not want to represent local or national things" with her collections. The clean garment lines allow for an emphasis on subtle differences in texture that remain unique to hand production. The resulting style is multi-national in the most factual sense of the word. Rather than the flattening of local difference as the media and consumers alike bemoan, Oma's multi-nationalism is about a sense of skill and care that draws the attention of customers in London

and Amsterdam, as well as Tokyo and Seoul.

From her atelier and showroom in Seoul, her mission is in part didactic. She admits that many customers are not familiar with the details of hand-produced textiles, but are curious to learn. Images and video footage are on hand to help teach new customers about the labour and knowledge behind the garments. A small loom on site allows for sampling, but also reminds customers that cloth does not just fall, fully formed, from the sky. Each collection rejects the relentless seasonal hunger of the fashion cycle. Instead she prefers to show once a year with a collection that covers spring to early autumn and keeps this calendar conspicuously out of season. Venues tend to be static exhibitions in galleries, rather than the thrum of the catwalk, and friends often act as the models.

"I am happy to show on this scale – I do not want to grow," she explains when I ask about the future. "When the brand grows, I cannot handle it myself. Small production with local artisans is something important that I believe in." Her stated desire to keep things small is understandable, but deceptively unusual. How often do we allow ourselves to say, next year I hope to be just about where I am now. In her case this is no mean feat. "Not many designers go this way – it is not an easy way," she admits. But craft is alive, understood as Chatwin observed, through touch. ••• **Jessica Hemmings**
www.omaspace.com

UP THE MOUNTAIN FOR DOWN

June Cashmere Unlocks a Kyrgyz Treasure Chest

In the jagged terrain of Southern Kyrgyzstan, the ancient Silk Road connecting East and West snakes its way through the Alai Mountain pass. Here, the Kyrgyz people live in quick-to-assemble yurts as semi-nomadic shepherds, herding Jaidari goats up the mountainside for summer and down again for winter. The work is difficult; many still plant and harvest their crops by hand or with horse-drawn ploughs. Yet in this rough beauty native goats produce a downy undercoat that is one of our finest textile fibres — cashmere.

The Kyrgyz do not keep the cashmere for themselves. Most recently, Asian companies have bought the fibre to mix with their own, thus hiding Kyrgyzstan's identity as a cashmere producer. While it seems ironic that one of the world's most rugged landscapes furnishes us with such a soft and warm fibre, it seems more paradoxical that in our global age, a country key to ancient trade has not been known for its exquisite natural resource by either the East or West. Until now.

There is a tradition in Kyrgyzstan in which a locked treasure chest of gifts is opened by daughters upon marriage. Whether brimming with family heirlooms or practical items, the opened chest symbolises the hope for prosperity. Similarly, June Cashmere of Ohio, USA, founded by Sy Belohlavek, allows Kyrgyz cashmere to be elevated in its own right to the world stage. By revitalizing shepherding and harvesting practices, June Cashmere exists to produce a sustainable line of highest quality cashmere yarn that is ecologically responsible, pays fair prices to the shepherds, and reinvests back into the local community. The company is, in essence, providing a Silk Road for Kyrgyzstan's identity in cashmere.

The inspiration for June Cashmere began in 2007 when a group of Kyrgyz artisans touring a small fibre mill in northeastern Ohio indicated that such a facility was needed in their home country. Intrigued, Sy spent the next two years in research. Superior quality cashmere requires particular genetics and husbandry techniques. The commodity is scarce as only the goat's soft, delicate undercoat is considered cashmere. It must be combed from the rougher outercoat during the spring moulting season and then sorted, by Kyrgyz women, to keep only the finest and longest fibres. Research by the Odessa Centre in England identified Kyrgyz goats are genetically capable of producing superior cashmere. Armed with this knowledge and the fact that a demand for inexpensive cashmere was fostering poor husbandry practices, land overuse and inferior quality, it became clear to Sy that Kyrgyzstan could gain its own identity in cashmere while restoring integrity to the market.

In 2013, Sy bought Osh Business and Training Center (OBTC) and began working on best breeding and harvesting practices with shepherds. He commissioned beautiful combs to be made and taught Kyrgyz families how to use them on the goats. Because of the lack of fibre processing infrastructure in-country, Sy sought facilities around the world, resulting in a 6,000 mile trek for the fibre to become yarn. The families meet up with Kanat Anarbaev from OBTC in the village streets and men conduct their trade in the back of a truck. June Cashmere purchases the fibre from the local center and the journey begins — scouring and sanitizing in Belgium, dehairing and milling in Great Britain, and organic dyeing in Maine, USA. At last it reaches Ohio for packaging and sales.

June Cashmere yarn has only been on the market for a year, expanding from a soft opening of a few colours to now a dozen naturally dyed hues. There are two weights of yarn in plies of three and six strands, allowing for incredible stitch definition in knitting. Being cashmere, the stitches bloom upon washing, showing off the softness of the fibre. It's no wonder that a high-end, hand-knit sweater company in New York City purchases the yarn to make a line of its products. The forecast already looks promising for June Cashmere: but for Sy, his efforts will have been for nought unless his families and investors realise a profit. He is in this (ad)venture also to give back. Sy said of the Kyrgyz families he works with, and in particular of his OBTC manager, "It's to empower the Kanats. That is why I want to do this." His ultimate dream would be for cashmere processing to take place in Kyrgyzstan to realize its full economic and social potential.

By producing yarn in which the betterment of Kyrgyz families is found in every skein, June Cashmere is a socially responsible rarity in the textile world. Restoring cashmere to its most pure and luxurious form in the process ensures that traditions and skills are not lost. Such an investment in people and resources surely demands support. ••• **Amy P. Swanson** www.junecashmere.com

Jared Heveron, Kirby Hsu, Ilya Tarasov

GO WITH THE FLOW

Annemarie O'Sullivan's aesthetics of movement

"The first time I wove with willow it was like swimming underwater; it's all about flow…" These striking words are from Annemarie O'Sullivan about her instant connection with the ancient skill of basket-making. It's a beguiling image, that something so rigid can represent flow: but one look at her exquisite work reveals exactly how fluid willow can be. Deeply elegant and somehow restrained, she combines rustic tradition with a modern aesthetic. This connection becomes more significant when I learn that she was a competitive swimmer in her youth. For her, weaving brought back those intense feelings of being continuously underwater. Her serious pursuit of willow weaving began by accident with a short course, unleashing further study and a dedicated obsession which became a business in 2011.

As we sit in her woodstove warmed studio, lovingly built by her partner Tom McWalter, she explains that this is a momentous day in that Tom has now officially joined her full-time as a collaborative partner in the willow weaving business. He is outside, meticulously bundling grades of willow together which have been harvested from their own plot, or rather 'osier' bed, nearby. She explains that at one time these osier willow beds would have been marked on an Ordnance Survey map and found scattered all over the countryside. As a basket-weaver it is traditional to manage your own coppiced willow, choosing from hundreds of available varieties with names like 'Dicky Meadows' and 'Dark Dicks': these willows are passed ceremoniously ▶

Alun Callender

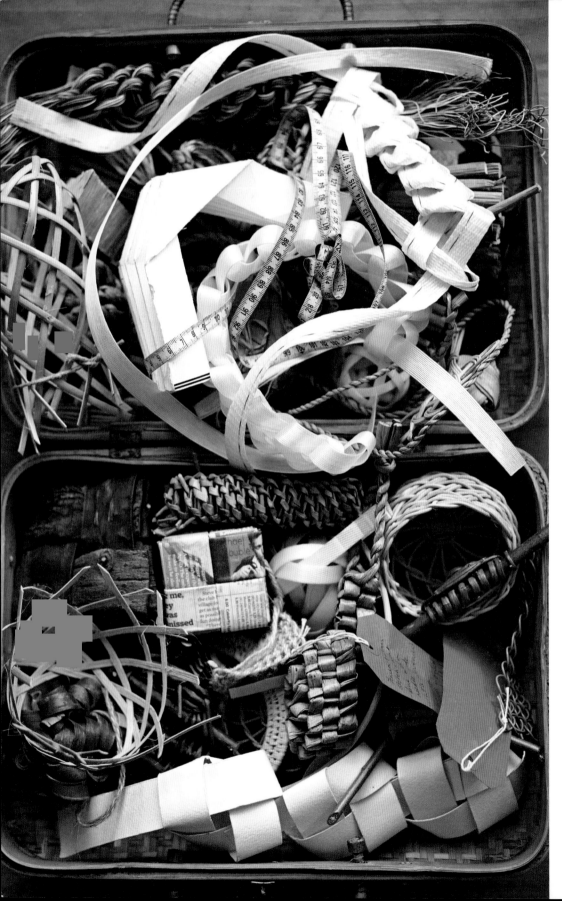

from maker to maker in the form of cuttings.

O'Sullivan knows the origin of her willow and that it has travelled through many soils and hands to reach her. Each year the slender, tall willow stems are cut back to nothing, only to regrow in full force the next year. The aim is for long stems which don't taper too much. The eternal question is whether to hide or celebrate the joins where one stem ends and the next begins. O'Sullivan seems especially good at these junctions, and the cut of the stem in itself often becomes a remarkable feature of her baskets.

This sense of place and being connected to the land permeates her work and O'Sullivan travels extensively, always learning and improving her skills — she has a rare openness to improving her knowledge. She describes this process of working with your hands as a series of constructions, twists, notches and fluid strokes; like sketching with wood. She calls it an 'aesthetic of movement' or even a 'dance': and much like swimming, it's the repetition and multiples of the process that create the momentum.

We talk in depth about the dynamics between functional and non-functional work. The great dilemma for basket weavers (and indeed many craftspeople) is the inherent functionality of the discipline. By definition baskets are functional and must employ certain characteristics to do their job successfully. A six month waiting list for her laundry baskets proves the point. Although

creating functional objects is deeply satisfying for O'Sullivan, there is another string to her bow and that is of a more architectural nature. Bigger in scale and more immersive, O'Sullivan created a series of finger-jointed, chestnut strip, spherical constructions for the Fabrica gallery in Brighton in 2011. These were created in response to an architectural technique called 'Grid Shell building' which was celebrating its tenth anniversary. Like the buildings, they were constructed flat and then 'hoisted' up to create three-dimensional curved, human-sized objects that meandered through the gallery space.

Behind this more playful and larger-scale work McWalter's influence can be felt. O'Sullivan reveals that they discuss making in great depth, and the opportunity to work together in a more concrete way is exciting. She hopes that this more monumental way of working will evolve further. His background in landscape design and the addition of another pair of full-time hands will mean that, together, they can build their practice in both functional and non-functional directions. Whatever the scale or end use the pieces may have in the future, there is an extraordinary sense of flow and calligraphic expertise already at play, endearing a new audience to appreciate this extraordinary craft. ••• **Ptolemy Mann**

Annemarie O'Sullivan will be teaching a basket-making course at Chateau Dumas, d'Auty, Nr Toulouse, 82220, France, 15-22 July 2017, for more details visit www.selvedge.org/events

LOFTY AMBITION

Fibre from the roof of the world

For centuries people have used animal hair or fleece for clothing without harming the animal who continues with its life. Such materials can be found in all sorts of wild terrains including the steppes, sierras and plateaux of the world's highest mountains. Tengri is a luxury, yet sustainable, fashion label designed in London and made in the UK and USA using natural, undyed yak fibre from central Mongolia's isolated mountainous Khangai region. It was founded in 2014: CEO Nancy Johnston trained as a social worker and lived with nomadic Mongolian herder families before setting up her company to perpetuate their community and culture. She is engaged in this ethical fairshare business with 4,500 nomadic herder families, thinking long term about conservation and the Mongolian environment – its people, traditions and ecology. 'Tengri' appropriately signifies the sky god that protects humans and the beauty of the earth.

Living above the snowline, the yak has a thick coat with shaggy, long hair. At the onset of winter it produces dense soft down as an extra layer of protection – this is collected by hand-combing once a year during the seasonal moult. Yak fibre has many inherent properties that make it desirable – lightweight, strong, insulating, breathable, elastic, hypoallergenic, lustrous, pill, odour and water resistant – it is ultimately weatherproof. Nancy Johnston has teamed up with Italian knitwear designer Carlo Volpi to make clothing and accessories using this precious material that is often compared to cashmere. The wonderful colouration of the indigenous semi-wild Kanghai yaks takes precedence as Tengri avoid damaging bleach and dye chemicals; preferring instead the natural colours ranging from the deepest blacks through chocolate browns, tans and greys to pure white and even (but rarely) gold. By keeping the Tengri label small and using mainly British manufacturers, Nancy can better oversee the spinning, knitting and tailoring processes. **www.tengri.co.uk** ▶

Norlha Textiles also use the look, feel and inherent properties of the yak fibre – from the Tibetan plateau known as the 'Roof of the World'. The name of the company references what the nomads call their yaks and is from the Tibetan phrase for 'wealth of the gods'. Kimberly Yeshi, founder/director, studied Anthropology and Buddhism while her daughter Dechen Yeshi, CEO has a background in Asian studies and film. Together they launched Norlha Textiles in 2007 with the aim of providing employment for the local Tibetans by promoting the use of yak fibre for the luxury market. Their signature look presents scarves, shawls and fashion where decoration is generally by way of stripes or checks.

The Norlha Textiles atelier is situated at 3,200 metres above sea level in the small village of Zorge Ritoma in north eastern Tibet's Amdo region – the 'Land of Snows' inhabited by nomads, yaks and sheep. The local textiles use the dense, soft under-fleece ('khullu') of the yak that is typically collected when the yak is two years old and the fibre at its best. This is spun, dyed (azo-free dyes) and then woven, knitted or felted – by hand into durable, lustrous, supple, snug and warm clothing and accessories of the highest quality.

Whereas Tengri work with the unadorned colour variations of the natural yak fibre Norlha Textiles dye it wonderful saturated hues. Their colours are inspired by the surrounding environment – bright reds, deep burgundies, fiery oranges and various shades of blue conjuring up the seemingly endless skies in this part of the world.

Working closely with the community, they respect the traditions and heritage of the local people while also borrowing textile traditions from other Asian cultures. Norlha Textiles supplies several Paris fashion houses including Lanvin, Balmain and Louis Vuitton as well as having their own brand. **www.norlhatextiles.com** ▸

Marcella Echavarrial

French-born architect Denis Colomb worked with several fashion boutiques in Paris, New York and Tokyo during the 1980s and 1990s before travelling to the Far East and Nepal where he became intrigued by the work of local artisans and Mongolian cashmere – reputably the finest in the world. In the early 2000s, while working on a collection of rugs for architectural commissions he started to experiment with this ultra-fine, super-soft fibre for accessories and went on to launch Los Angeles-based 'Denis Colomb Lifestyle' in 2004 with his wife – well-known photographer Erica Lennard.

The products are designed in California and hand woven in small, fairtrade Kathmandu workshops with the couple frequently travelling to Nepal to oversee production. The label includes luxurious scarves, wraps and clothing for both men and women, with collections shown by appointment four times a year in Paris. Being cashmere they are featherweight and give non-bulky warmth when layered – ensuring the wearer stays comfortable even in persistent air-conditioning. They also pack-up small making them ideal for global travel.

The range of garments and accessories impart a beautifully fluid casual elegance and come undyed in the natural shades of the fleece or in a bold monochrome palette or in a myriad of vivid colours – colour-blocked, tie-dyed, two-tone or even reversible. Furthermore geometric patterning such as broad and narrow stripes, plaids, herringbone, chevron and zig-zag patterns attest to his architectural background. Either in pure cashmere or in cashmere blends with silk or linen the impeccable quality products of Denis Colomb Lifestyle have a unisex appeal - desired by all who adore their wrap-around comfort, enveloping sensuality and general sumptuousness.••• **Sarah E. Braddock Clarke** **www.deniscolomb.com**

Erica Lennard

FREE KAFFE FASSETT COSMETICS

Three-year subscribers... Receive a complimentary cosmetic set designed by Kaffe Fassett

Enter the colourful world of Kaffe Fassett through his bespoke fragrance. Known for his colourful textile designs, Kaffe Fassett has applied his eye to cosmetics. Working with the brand Heathcote & Ivory, Kaffe has created a beautiful, high quality collection of pieces to brighten up your day. We have one hundred gifts, each worth £53, to give away to the first one hundred three-year subscribers. Each gift comprises an On Point Cosmetic Bag – worth £18. Inspired by Jacobean tapestry the bag features Kaffe's floral needlepoint design. Also included are a set of On Point Collective Hand Creams, worth £10 and an Essential Achillea Kit, in his signature floral design worth £25. Call or visit **www.selvedge.org** to subscribe. **www.kaffefassettfragrance.com**

SUBSCRIBING TO SELVEDGE IS EASY...

by phone: T: +44 (0)20 8341 9721

by post: COMPLETE THE FORM OPPOSITE AND SEND TO: SELVEDGE, 162 ARCHWAY ROAD, LONDON, N6 5BB, UK

online: WWW.SELVEDGE.ORG

Subscribe now...

NAME OF SUBSCRIBER/CARD HOLDER:

TITLE:

NAME: SURNAME:

ADDRESS:

COUNTRY: POSTCODE/ZIP:

HOME TEL:

EMAIL (VERY IMPORTANT):

I WOULD LIKE TO SEND A GIFT SUBSCRIPTION TO:

TITLE:

NAME: SURNAME:

ADDRESS:

COUNTRY: POSTCODE/ZIP:

HOME TEL:

EMAIL (VERY IMPORTANT):

PLEASE START ◯ RENEW ◯ MY SUBSCRIPTION FROM ISSUE [ ]   PLEASE SEND FIRST COPY TO GIFT RECIPIENT ◯ PURCHASER ◯

SUBSCRIPTIONS: STANDARD

REGION	6 Months 3 issues	1 Year 6 issues	2 Years 12 issues	3 Years 18 issues
UK	◯ £27.50	◯ £50.00	◯ £90.00	◯ £125.00
EUROPE	◯ £40.00	◯ £75.00	◯ £135.00	◯ £190.00
REST OF WORLD	◯ £55.00	◯ £100.00	◯ £180.00	◯ £250.00

CONTINUOUS

6 months 3 issues	1 Year 6 issues
◯ £25.00	◯ £45.00
◯ £36.00	◯ £67.50
◯ £50.00	◯ £90.00

BY ISSUE

2 months 1 issue
◯ £9.95
◯ £13.45
◯ £17.95

DIGITAL

Digital subscriptions and back issues are available for **£39.95 per year** and **£9.95** respectively. For full details visit **www.selvedge.org**

ALREADY A SUBSCRIBER? TELL A FRIEND, RECEIVE A FREE ISSUE*

Add your details below, pass this form to a friend. *If they subscribe we'll add an extra issue to your subscription.

NAME: SURNAME:

POSTCODE/ZIP:

Available on the **App Store**

PAYMENT DETAILS - PLEASE ENSURE ALL REQUIRED FIELDS ARE COMPLETED

◯ **PayPal** PLEASE SEND INVOICE TO EMAIL:

◯ Credit Card (COMPLETE OPPOSITE)   AMOUNT:

◯ Cheque (PAYABLE TO SELVEDGE LTD)   AMOUNT:

◯ Bank Transfer* UK Customers only   AMOUNT:

REF**: SELVEDGE - _ _ _ _ _ _ _ _ - _ _ / _ _ / _ _

CARD TYPE: ◯ MasterCard ◯ VISA ◯ VISA ELECTRON ◯ Maestro

CARD NUMBER: [ ][ ][ ][ ] [ ][ ][ ][ ] [ ][ ][ ][ ] [ ][ ][ ][ ]

CVV NUMBER (LAST 3 DIGITS): [ ][ ][ ]   SWITCH ISSUE NUMBER: [ ]

START DATE [ ][ ] / [ ][ ]   EXPIRY DATE: [ ][ ] / [ ][ ]

CARDHOLDER'S SIGNATURE: DATE:

** PLEASE USE A REFERENCE FOR YOUR TRANSFER SO WE CAN ALLOCATE THE PAYMENT. WE SUGGEST USING 'SELVEDGE - POSTCODE - DATE OF TRANSFER'

Subscription Terms & Conditions: We aim to dispatch your first copy as quickly as possible but in certain circumstances or if your address is outside of the UK the first issue of your subscription may take up to 6 weeks to arrive. You can cancel your Selvedge subscription at any time. To do so please contact subscriptions@selvedge.org. A continuous subscription to Selvedge means your subscription will be automatically renewed when the final issue of the subscription has been dispatched. If you have selected a 3 issue continuous subscription, a payment will be taken once the third issue has been dispatched. For a 6 issue continuous subscription, payment will be taken once the sixth issue has been dispatched. The agreement can be cancelled at any time by informing Selvedge in writing. We require 30 days notice. A refund will be made less the cover price of any dispatched issues. If your payment is rejected for any reason your subscription will not be automatically renewed. Missing issues will only be replaced if claimed within three months of publication.

*Paying by BACS transfer saves you money in bank charges and helps Selvedge to reduce its costs. If you would prefer to pay by BACS please use the information provided: **Name:** Selvedge **Bank:** Lloyds **Account Number:** 0219 3986 **Sort Code:** 309380 **IBAN:** GB54 LYOD 3093 8002 1939 86 **SWIFT:** LOYDGB21065

NB: Subscription and back issue prices are correct at time of going to press and valid until 28/02/17

COMPLETE YOUR COLLECTION

issue 00 - £16.95 ○   issue 01 - £11.95 ○   issue 02 - £16.95 ○   issue 04 - £11.95 ○   issue 06 - £6.95 ○   issue 07 - £16.95 ○   issue 08 - £11.95 ○   issue 10 - £11.95 ○   issue 11 - £11.95 ○   issue 12 - £11.95 ○   issue 13 - £16.95 ○   issue 14 - £6.95 ○

issue 15 - £6.95 ○   issue 16 - £16.95 ○   issue 18 - £16.95 ○   issue 19 - £6.95 ○   issue 20 - £11.95 ○   issue 23 - £6.95 ○   issue 24 - £28.95 ○   issue 26 - £6.95 ○   issue 28 - £11.95 ○   issue 34 - £11.95 ○   issue 36 - £11.95 ○   issue 37 - £16.95 ○

issue 38 - £11.95 ○   issue 39 - £11.95 ○   issue 40 - £11.95 ○   issue 46 - £6.95 ○   issue 47 - £16.95 ○   issue 48 - £11.95 ○   issue 49 - £16.95 ○   issue 50 - £16.95 ○   issue 51 - £11.95 ○   issue 52 - £11.95 ○   issue 54 - £28.95 ○   issue 56 - £11.95 ○

issue 59 - £16.95 ○   issue 60 - £16.95 ○   issue 61 - £11.95 ○   issue 62 - £16.95 ○   issue 63 - £16.95 ○   issue 64 - £16.95 ○   issue 65 - £16.95 ○   issue 67 - £11.95 ○   issue 68 - £11.95 ○   issue 69 - £16.95 ○   issue 71 - £11.95 ○   issue 72 - £11.95 ○

ORDER ALL AVAILABLE BACK ISSUES OF SELVEDGE (48 ISSUES @ £6 each) **Free P&P.** Email customerservice@selvedge.org

FOLD HERE

FOLD HERE

FOLD OVER HERE

2

SELVEDGE
FREEPOST NAT 10681
LONDON
N6 5BR

THERE ARE 3 WAYS TO PAY 1 ON OUR WEBSITE: WWW.SELVEDGE.ORG 2 BY PHONE: +44 (0) 20 8341 9721 3 BY POST: 162 ARCHWAY ROAD LONDON N6 5BR

WIN, WIN, WIN

Exclusively for Selvedge Readers ... visit www.selvedge.org to enter

The Shop Floor Project is offering readers the chance to win three pieces from their most popular collections: the wool and silk Botanical Inlay shawl, 140x140cm, worth £125, a hand-beaten brass Wall Sconce by Malin Appelgren, worth £265 and a print from the 17th Century Paint Chart series, 30x21cm, worth £65. The Shop Floor Project is excited to have been granted permission to create a limited edition print collection from the pages of this remarkable book. **www.theshopfloorproject.com**

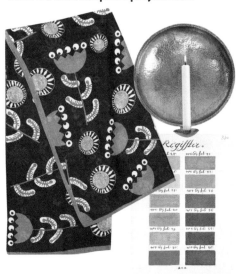

To enter please visit www.selvedge.org

Annemarie O'Sullivan makes baskets and woven objects, which are a response to the materials she hand gathers from the land. She grows twenty different types of willow and often combines these with coppiced wood. Annemarie is passionate about seeing the making process through from source to finished piece – ensuring her feet stay on the earth. Her work draws on the sturdiness of agricultural baskets, the curves of the landscape and a deep respect for ancient crafts. She is inspired by the simple connections that she has with basket-makers from the past. This kindling basket, worth £310, is woven from Somerset willow and has an integral coppiced hazel handle. Measuring 50cm in height and just over 30cm in diameter, this is a great basket to use to gather and store kindling, **www.annemarieosullivan.co.uk**

Jo Crowther

Tengri champions sustainable manufacturing, using noble fibres. These are hand-combed from an indigenous breed of yak, in the Khangai region of Mongolia, which has less impact on biodiversity than non-indigenous and domesticated animal species introduced and bred for their fibres. Tengri works directly with 4,500 nomadic herder families, ensuring a fair share income whilst establishing herders' land rights and offering consumers a 100% transparent supply chain. More than just a luxury label, Tengri is a brand built by people unwilling to settle for the status quo. The Tengri duo-purpose throw worth £225 functions as an everyday cover-up and travel accessory that will last a lifetime. Woven with precious noble yarns from the Mongolian Khangai yak in a heritage British mill, and hand finished in London, this 100% natural, undyed scarf is as soft as cashmere, warmer than merino wool, hypoallergenic and water-resistant. **www.tengri.co.uk**

Yokainoshima is a very unusual book and a must-have for any cultural aficionado. French photographer Charles Fréger has had a long career exploring different ways in which communities around the world come together. In his research about European tradition he learned of a connection with Japanese expressions. This journey took him to Akita where he discovered Namahage, a deity that appears before the new year searching for lazy children. From this initial interest, a two-year book project took him all over Japan to re-imagine these living creatures.

Yokainoshima is a catalogue of Yokai or monsters in Japanese folklore through the eyes of Charles Fréger. The book flows like a dance of characters who come and go, beautifully attired mostly with masks and customes made of Japanese textiles and natural fibres. There are cultural references to every image in the back of the book, explaining how the concerns of daily life are dealt with in a poetic way by Japanese society. For example, there are monsters coming to bless the harvests and others who console the bereaved. There are also many rituals relating to longevity, prosperity and warding off misfortune. In Japanese mythology and folklore, the Yōkai are eclectic spirits, monsters, or demons. They can be malevolent or mischievous in character, bewitching, beguiling, mysterious creatures of a supernatural world. Most commonly, they are shapeshifters, taking on an array of forms including animals, ogres, goblins, household objects, and grotesque humans. However, Charles makes it clear that Yokainoshima is an island of monsters that exists only in his imagination. He has claimed not to be an anthropologist.

The settings chosen by Charles are Japanese landscapes upon which the creatures in costumes are juxtaposed. The insular aspect of Japan comes out with the presence of the sea and the rugged mountainous landscape. If one noun had to be chosen to describe the production, it would be cleanliness. There are hardly any shadows and the monsters are shown in bright daylight. The creatures themselves are in total control of their movements and gestures, posing as if in a trance or caught in the middle of a dramatic movement or gesture. The fact that this research into folklore, tradition and the

invisible comes to light in the form of contemporary photography adds yet another layer to the project. As Toshiharu Ito says in the book, one of the aims of photography is to capture eternity. Charles's point of view speaks of the past, the present and, especially, the future. A bestiary of kinds. ••• **Marcella Echavarria: Yokainoshima: Island of Monsters, Japanese Folk Rituals, Charles Fréger £25 Thames & Hudson, ISBN 9780500544594. To order your copy at the special price of £18.95 inc UK mainland delivery (overseas prices available on request) please call Littlehampton Book Services on 01903 828503, quoting "TH284". Offer is subject to availability and runs until 31 March 2017.**

BOOKS

Appearances are often deceptive so if you expect this book to simply be a survey of Afghani rugs and carpets you will be mistaken. It is more an intriguing glimpse of Afghan life told through the history of it's textiles. Working for a British Mining Company, the author, Richard Parsons was posted to Tehran where he fell in love with Oriental Carpets. Abandoning this steady job he became a knowledgeable authority on carpets of the region, travelling extensively throughout Afghanistan before the Russian invasion of 1979. This scholarly book shares the history, the culture and a way of life that has all but disappeared.

There are plenty of glossy images of a wide variety of classic rugs; felted, stitched, and all weaving styles, documented in fascinating detail. They are placed geographically, described by the wool type and handle, dyes used, styles of weaving and the significant characteristics. But for me the precious, black and white photographs expose the real life of the people. Chapter five treats us to vivid descriptions of the Carpet Bazaars. We are told that a canny dealer would check the state of the Livestock market as an indicator of fiscal buoyancy before venturing to buy carpets. The etiquette of securing a sale is surprising formal. Should the haggling falter it was commonplace for an independent onlooker to intervene and help conclude the transaction. The price having been agreed both parties would hold the cash, give it three upward shakes of the hand to seal the deal.

Other market day activities such as the slaughter of animals are detailed including the graphic procedure of nicking a goat's leg, blowing into the carcass, to facilitate the separation of the skin from the flesh. Priceless.

The final chapter covers the plight of Afghani refugees. It is sobering that refugee artisans were thwarted in their carpet making by the scarcity of good dyestuffs. Skilled weavers settled in Pakistan, Turkey and Iran managing to continue their work despite hostile conditions and directives from dealers who encouraged them to produce simplified designs for westerners. Parsons is clearly scathing about this activity. The final haunting words of the book, originally written in 1983, question how these people will fare when they can return to Afghanistan. How and when indeed?

This is a delightful written book to dip into to discover a hidden world. ••• **Helen Yardley The Carpets of Afghanistan, Richard D. Parsons, ACC Art Books, £45, ISBN: 9781851497904. For a 35% discount off the publication price simply register with the publisher's website, www.accdistribution.com and enter the promotional code ACC35 upon purchase, or call the UK office on +44 (0)1394 389 977**

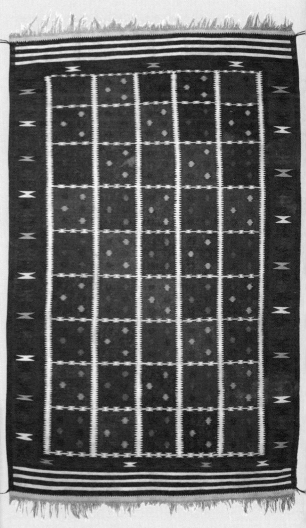

VIEW

On the Grid: Textiles and Minimalism, 23 July 2016 - 12 February 2017, de Young Museum, Golden Gate Park, 50 Hagiwara Tea Garden Drive, San Francisco, CA 94118, www.deyoung.famsf.org

The legendary weaver Anni Albers wrote in *On Weaving* (1965) : "It is safe, I suppose, to assume that today most if not all of us have had the experience of looking down from an airplane onto this earth. What we see is a free flow of forms intersected here and there by straight lines, rectangles, circles, and evenly drawn curves; that is, by shapes of great regularity. Here we have, then, natural and man made forms in contradistinction. And here before us we can recognize the essence of designing, a visually comprehensive, simplified organization of forms that is distinct from nature's secretive and complex working." Albers continues: "To turn from 'looking at' to action: we grow cabbages in straight rows and are not tempted by nature's fanciful way of planting to scatter them freely about. Always, though sometimes in a way that is roundabout and apparent only as an underlying theme of composition, it is clarity that we seek. But when the matter of usefulness is involved, we plainly and without qualification use our characteristics: forms that, however they may deviate in their final development, are intrinsically geometric."

Of course we remember that she, and husband Joseph Albers, were at the forefront of the 'modernist revolution' in the 20s and 30s; he with his colour analysis; she with her focus on structure; both getting to the essence of visual perception and structural phenomena. That new 'minimalism' was a relief from the overly ornate Victorian age and its excesses at the end of the nineteenth century. It was also a departure from the rampantly organic Art Nouveau period that followed.

And so *On the Grid* reminds us again of those ageless principles and understandings; those basic structural elements and processes that create textiles, first as utilitarian objects that sustain life, and then as spiritual embodiments of philosophies, aesthetic theories, religious beliefs. The exhibition encompasses these universalities of textiles by including twenty-seven examples from across world cultures that celebrate the fundamental attributes dictated by the loom, where warp and weft intersect at right angles. From simple, plain rectangular shawls and loin cloths, the show expands to include a sixteenth century Buddhist priest robe and a tunic from Burma, all rectangular garments. Slowly, pattern is added into the exhibition through the use of stripes, plaids and checkerboards, all natural results achieved in the weaving process. Embellishments also occur as part of the weaving process through the use of gold leaf paper that wraps individual yarns and combines with those that are space-dyed ikat (kasuri) in a small eighteenth century fragment from Japan.

Freer patterning is achieved on an example of bark cloth (siapo) from Polynesia, specifically Samoa. Basically, because bark cloth is a paper made of mulberry bark, there could be fewer limitations to adding pattern by direct painting, although traditionally the designs are usually geometric patterns. The fundamental structure of bark cloth itself is created from slabs of the material layered in alternating right angles to strengthen the structure, and then pounded together. Essentially, the same warp and weft principle is used, but without a loom. Bark cloth, like felt and other non-wovens, is based on moisture and pressure, rather than interlocking threads. The most decorated piece is a Japanese Buddhist altar cloth (uchishiki) from the early nineteenth century that incorporates gold leaf paper strips wrapped around threads in supplementary-weft patterning (kinran) that forms a repeated pattern of large, abstracted plum blossoms in the 10x10cm base cloth. The single contemporary "art" piece is a large rectangular hanging entitled *Wall of Windows*, 1990, by American Rebecca R. Medel. Of cotton and linen, it incorporates knotted netting and warp and weft-resist dyeing (ikat). The traditional net structure serves a different purpose from those used by fishermen for centuries; but it is the same, ageless grid structure that helped to feed thousands of people for thousands of years.

This exhibition is a meditation, a room full of calm, orderly forms that reassert the fundamental principles of structure based on rational simplicity; the essence of minimalism achieved through calm, orderly, mathematical systems; a bit of welcome relief from our hectic world. ••• **Jo Ann C. Stabb Left: Married woman's shoulder cloth (lawon), 1900 Palembang, Sumatra. Silk; stitch-resist dyeing (tritik), 205 x 78cm Right: Quilt: "Checkerboard" pattern, ca.1900. United States, Indiana, Amish. Cotton, wool. 188 x 200cm**

VIEW

VIEW

Cary Wolinsky: Fiber of Life, 8 October 2016
- 28 February 2017, Fuller Craft Museum,
455 Oak Street, Brockton, MA 02301,
www.fullercraft.org

Taking you across continents and cultures where the camera captures the transformative power of cloth is Cary Wolinsky's installation of images at the Fuller Craft Museum. The venue is a perfect complement to the Wolinsky installation because its commitment to contemporary craft is unique to New England. Fuller's motto "let the art touch you", in other words keep work accessible to all, is consistent in its exhibitions, demonstrations, and workshops. The installation consists of archival inkjet images that are part of a much larger series that was on view at Pucker Gallery in Boston in 2007 and for which there was a small catalogue produced. In spite of the Fuller installation being only ten images, they are profoundly moving and a well edited narrative of discovery and passion for the subject matter.

Cary Wolinsky was a career photographer for the publication National Geographic. While he was on assignment in Varanasi India, he had a surreptitious encounter in a carpet-weaving village where he witnessed people engaged in spinning wool. That moment in 1972 was captured on film becoming *The Spinner* Bhadohi, India and is the second image in the exhibition. *The Spinner* was the genesis for what became a decades long passion for textiles and fashion for Wolinsky. The encounter in India was also the catalyst for what would become two major features for The National Geographic: ▶

Fuller Craft Museum

VIEW

the first *Silk* in 1984, and later *Wool* in 1986. The magazine was surprised when *Silk* became its most popular feature ever, and that led to Wolinsky being assigned the follow-up story on wool. Both of these stories took Wolinksy around the world, and it was through the silk project that he met and worked with the late great fashion editor for the Washington Post, Nina Hyde. Wolinsky had never paid any mind to fashion prior to working with Hyde on the silk project, and to this day Cary recognizes the significance of textiles and clothing. Wolinsky's own eloquent words on the topic make up the introductory panel in the gallery;"Textiles are rich 'material' for stories. Embedded like DNA in the threads that form their warp and weft are stories about culture, politics, innovation, intrigue, greed, massive fortunes, and environmental collapse. What has drawn and held my attention as a photographer, however, is that a single piece of cloth can express light and movement texture and volume, even emotion. It can be a projection of self or obfuscation: a disguise behind which to mislead the viewer. Cloth has the power to define and transform our impression of another human being."

The photographs on view have an ethereal and painterly quality, maybe simply because of the subject matter, but I think it is something more. Taken between 1972-1997 and varying from editorialized to moment in time or action shots, Wolinsky composes his subjects with striking arrangements of colour and light so that the subject becomes more than simply documenting a process or an object such as a sari or cloth seller. He is able to capture the essence whether it is a half shorn sheep in Australia, or a funeral cloth seller in Ghana by his choice of perspective, whether it be front and centre or low angle, natural versus spot lighting, or something more atmospheric: but every image reads as a timeless and universal portrait of life in which cloth becomes the common language.

The final image happens to be from his time working with Nina Hyde in Paris reporting on the couture shows for National Geographic silk project. He was interested in capturing the ambiance of the fashion shows more so than the individual models, and his distinctive perspective again is visible in the shot of *The Wedding Dress* taken at the Musee Louvre. The wedding dress has been the traditional finale of a designer's collection, and Wolinsky has captured this out of this world moment akin to the second coming or at least with a nod to the divine which coincidentally concludes the *Fiber of Life* exhibition as well. This and the other nine images turn out to be extremely powerful communicators. *Fiber of Life* is a brief encounter with an artist/photographer whose point of view of a subject he initially discovers by accident and then becomes an avid storyteller and ambassador.

In addition to being a contributor to National Geographic Wolinsky has been a regular contributor to American Craft Magazine for the past four years. ••• **Joanne Dolan Ingersoll Previous page, left: Pilgrims Cloth, Mathura, UP, India, Previous Page right: Funeral Cloth Seller, Accra, Ghant, Half Shorn Sheep, Beaufort, Victoria, Australia.**

Fiji: Art & Life in the Pacific, 15 October - 12 February 2017, The Sainsbury Centre for Visual Arts, University of East Anglia, Norwich, Norfolk, NR4 7TJ, www.scva.ac.uk

Fijian masi or bark cloth is one of the most versatile fabrics in the Pacific — and it plays an integral part in culture and the Fijian way of life. A new exhibition at the Sainsbury Centre reveals hitherto unknown facets of this beautiful textile.

Barkcloth is a unique material. It has been hand made in Fiji for generations and is very much a family business. The cloth is still made today using traditional methods. Bark cloth is derived from young mulberry trees, which local people grow in plantations. When the tree is deemed old enough, it is cut down. All the outside bark is removed and only the inside fibre is used to make barkcloth. This fibre is carefully peeled away, soaked and and then left to dry in the sun. A group of family members then work together to fold and beat the cloth, time and time again until the required thickness is achieved. It may be thick and opaque or even turned into delicate, gauzy strands of transparent gossamer.

Creating the textile and decorating the textiles is a community activity. It is also a female one. Even the words used to describe the process are female orientated, as Project Administrator Katrina Taleilgglesden explains."The mulberry tree is seen as the creator of life, while the inner bark is the flesh which bleeds releasing pink liquid when beaten. Every thing about bark cloth relates to the giving of life."

VIEW

Hand painting and stenciling are the most common forms of ornamentation, using ornate abstract designs which occasionally include recognizable objects – added simply because the designers liked the shape of the object. Typical of this is a nineteenth century bark cloth that includes musket images. Colours are limited in scope to reds and blacks, reflecting the natural materials available on the islands. Black comes from the soot of the candlenut tree, while reds vary in shade from deep reds to shades which are almost golden brown depending on the island location from which the red clay is derived. Individual locations can be identified by the style of design being used. For example, islands closer to Tonga tended to use a rubbing style method of decoration in which the colour was rubbed on the cloth revealing the pattern held on a wooden board under the fabric.

Barkcloths are extremely prestigious items within Fijian culture and can be very large. The SCVA exhibition contains examples that are over fifteen metres long. Within Fiji, barkcloth is still used and given as gifts, just as it has been for hundreds of years. Within the home, barkcloth is used for bedding, to create screens and wall hangings, as mosquito curtains and ceremonial clothing. It is usually given as a gift for special people such as chiefs, new babies, or weddings. The barkcloth is given in a very distinctive way. The recipient is often wrapped in layers of barkcloth which may be wound round and round, or looped up around the body. The bigger the barkcloth, the longer the train, the more prestigious is the gift. "There are accounts of people being wrapped in such a ▶

Museum of Archaeology and Anthropology, University of Cambridge

massive length of barkcloth, that assistants have to stand on either side to support them as they walk," recounts Katrina. The exhibtion includes a beautiful example of ceremonial attire which could be worn by either sex. The three piece outfit is decorated with reddish brown stencils, and even the garland is made out of barkcloth flowers.

Barkcloth has now become a fashion textile following the decision of Adi Litia Mara to use the fabric for her wedding dress in 1991. As she was marrying an Englishman, Lord Henry Dugdale, she wanted to combine elements of both heritages. A NZ fashion designer was commissioned to create a western style wedding dress using barkcloth grown and made on her mother's plantation in Vanua. The dress also contained decorative symbols paying homage to Adi's father's family, and a tiny blue scroll hidden in the bustle reflecting the western idea of 'something blue'. The white 'chiefly' colour reflected her importance on her wedding day, as did the long train. The result was phenomenal. It set off an enduring fashion trend for designer barkcloth wedding dresses. Designers began looking more closely at this fabric, which in the humid Pacific climate is very malleable and flexible. It is now a mainstay of many a couture collection. ••• **Angela Youngman**
Right: Barkcloth (detail) Fiji, c. 1850 – 1859 bark cloth and pigment 160 x 1213 cm
Left: Long decorated barkcloth sheet, masi bolabola (detail). Fiji. 1870s. Paper mulberry, pigment. 758 cm. Collected in the 1870s. Highly prized and extremely prestigious, barkcloth and its designs are now part of the Fijian national identity.

.

Trustees of the Fiji Museum

Kimsooja: Archive of Mind, 27 July 2016 – 5 February 2017, National Museum of Modern and Contemporary Art, Seoul, South Korea, www.mmca.go.kr

Kimsooja has long explored meditative approaches to her artistic practice. Textile enthusiasts may be most familiar with her use of the wrapping cloth she calls Bottari in various projects or her film *Needle Woman*. In the latter we see the artist's back, her stance stationary while crowds in various locations around the world stream past her – some faces curious, others oblivious. Over several decades of artistic work Kimsooja has treated the textile as fundamentally pedestrian. In many ways so is this latest exhibition content. But while the exhibition press release refers to "the artist's early meditation on non-doing and non-making as a form of art practice", her current exhibition in Seoul turns doing and making over to the public.

Centre-stage is *Archive of Mind* (2016). After patiently queuing (testament to the exhibition's popularity with the public) visitors are counted in to a low lit room and invited to roll balls of clay. Four distinct shades of clay dominate the slowly drying landscape. An audio titled *Unfolding Sphere, sounds of* the artist gurgling and rolling clay, plays while queuing. But the space is dominated not by the audio, but by an elliptical wooden table nineteen metres in length filled with the ant-like efforts of the public. Each day builds a record of individual hands learning – through an opportunity to do rather than observe – that something as simple as rolling clay into a sphere isn't in fact easy to do.

Photo by Aaron Wax, Courtesy of MMCA and Hyundai Motor Co. and Kimsooja Studio

VIEW

This is where the rub with this fascinating exhibition begins. Simple, repetitive activities are presented as a gateway to a clearer, calmer way of thinking. The physical outputs are modest enough to cast doubt on their purpose. But visitors are clearly mesmerised by the invitation. The installation has proven popular enough that the clay spheres have to be regularly collected and stored to provide more room on the table. The artist has mentioned plans to kiln fire this public effort, both to keep dust to a minimum and make storage of the archive practical. And while my two wonky contributions surely mean nothing, the collective record that spread across the table undeniably presents its own beauty.

Archive of Mind could be read as the antithesis of Chinese artist Ai Wei Wei's *Sunflower Seeds* (2010-11) installed in the Tate Modern Turbine Hall: unskilled play set in distinct contrast to the anonymous, albeit individual, labour. The contrast may be unintentional, but in both cases simplicity proved a powerful draw for the viewing public. And in both cases material misbehaviour plays a part. Ai Wei Wei's original invitation for the public to walk over the carpet of ceramic seeds was quashed by health and safety concerns about the amount of dust this created.

After wiping the traces of clay from your hands, visitors move into a much smaller but equally intimate space to be faced with the artist's yoga mat patterned through the dedicated wear of practice. The mat is wall mounted and displayed alongside a digitally embroidered sound bite of her breath on stretched silk. Again it is the pedestrian that dominates – but crucially Kimsooja's pedestrian. (I'm quite sure my yoga mat would find no welcome home in a public art space.) In the final gallery a video installation moves between images of swirling muddied water from the south west of the United States – a potter's wheel inverted as slip eddies inward; aerial photographs of the landscape etched by water over time that would not look out of place in an American National Park pamphlet; and imagery of women basket weaving and carding fibres.

How Kimsooja's invitation of public labour to roll clay spheres, the artistic significance of her well worn yoga mat or film footage of basket weaving and carding fibres make for a comfortable fit in the Museum of Modern and Contemporary Art is a tantalising question. Part of the answer lies in their combination. And part may lie with Kimsooja's creative identity, which embraces much of what we could call craft ideals – but with less interest in what the material can be than in the meditative states that repetitive action might bring about.

In amongst all those clay balls made by public invitation are my efforts: two stubborn triangles of clay that I swear looked nothing like all the other endeavours left on the table. Craft can be humbling. But the irony, considering Kimsooja's interest in mindfulness, is that misbehaving materials can also be downright irritating. ••• **Jessica Hemmings**
Right and Left: Kimsooja, Archive of Mind, 2016, participatory site specific installation

COMING NEXT

The Endeavour issue: Hard working textiles

OUT 10 FEBRUARY

*Contents are subject to change.

Print to Order Early printed textiles

True Blue What makes a colour utilitarian

A Life in Objects Inside the home of Emery Walker

Social History The forgotten textile mills in America

Painting Industry The depiction of workwear by Lowry, Spencer and more

Plus: Smocks, Baskets, Chris Ofili, The Industrial Revolution, Neisha Crosland

Christopher Payne

SUBSCRIBE AND SAVE Turn to page 81 for full details or visit www.selvedge.org

Dating possibly as far back as Neolithic times, felt is one of the most ancient forms of textile. Thought to have been inspired by the natural process of felting, early shepherds gathered the clumpy knots that naturally formed in the fleeces of their sheep, and washed, rolled, and shaped them to create the first felt cloth. It was only a small step further to manage the process by shearing and cleaning the wool first, before felting it by hand by agitating the fibres to cause the scales coating each strand to mesh together.

Although felt is found throughout central Asia, Europe, South America and North Africa, Burel felt from the Serra de Estrela Mountains in Portugal dates back to the twelfth century when it was worn by Franciscan monks. Burel felt is unusual because the fibre is spun and woven into a coarse cloth first, before being scalded with hot water and pummelled to compound it into shape making it more resilient. Similar to Loden cloth from the Tyrolean Mountains, and in a parallel tradition, Burel was originally worn by the region's shepherds who needed a fabric that would withstand the rugged terrain as well as the extreme mountain climate. They fashioned all-encompassing capes from Burel, which were warm and water resistant, and later became known as the Portuguese Capote.

The Burel tradition was modernised during the nineteenth century when the cloth went into factory production, but began to diminish in the twentieth century. By the time that Isabel Dias da Costa and João Tomás came across the Império Wool factory in the Serra de Estrela Mountains in 2006, it had been abandoned for many years. Enchanted by the Burel tradition, and rich with innovation, they were determined to revive the business, using the factory's antique machines and the skills of the local artisans. Their vision in a spectrum of vibrant shades sees the felt pinched, folded and layered in a library of geometric and structural forms to create fascinating wall coverings, soft furnishings and bags. And whilst the original wearers – the Franciscan monk and the mountain shepherd – might be overwhelmed by Burel in cerise magenta or electric blue, the floral and foliate designs inspired by the natural environment – such as the folded channels of the 'Leivas' design that resembles the furrows of a ploughed field and the crosses of the 'Cruz' – would be reassuringly familiar in their simple beauty. ••• **Sarah Jane Downing** **www.burelfactory.com**

SWATCH
Favourite fabric No.34: Burel

Georgina McAusland